RUGBY LEAGUE JOURNAL ANNUAL 2009

RUGBY LEAGUE JOURNAL
PUBLISHING

First published in Great Britain in 2008 by
Rugby League Journal Publishing
P.O. Box 22, Egremont, Cumbria, CA23 3WA

ISBN 978-09548355-4-5

Edited and designed by Harry Edgar

Sales and Marketing by Ruth Edgar

Printed by Printexpress (Cumbria) Limited

Front cover pictures:
Main picture: Sam Burgess playing for Great Britain.
(Photograph by courtesy of Andrew Varley Picture Agency)
Inset pictures: Shaun Long, Jason Robinson, Rob Burrow.
Andy Gregory and Ellery Hanley playing for Great Britain.
(Photograph by courtesy of Eddie Whitham).
Frontispiece picture:
Jackie Merquey playing for France versus Australia at Bordeaux in 1956.

RUGBY LEAGUE JOURNAL
PUBLISHING

P.O. Box 22, Egremont, Cumbria, CA23 3WA
E-Mail: rugbyleague.journal@virgin.net   Telephone: 01946 814249
www.rugbyleaguejournal.net

CONTENTS

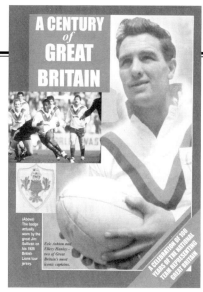

This Annual continues a 12-page special section paying tribute to a Century of the Great Britain team.

As we pay tribute to a Century of the Great Britain team in this book, we believe no man represented their spirit better and with more dignity than Trevor Foster - pictured in action as a member of the *"Indomitables"* touring team in 1946. As a player, and for the rest of his life as a member of the Lions Association, Trevor represented Great Britain with the pride and sportsmanship we hope all future generations can be inspired by.

Our thanks to all the photographers whose skills have provided so many fine images in this book. With so many old pictures from private collections it is often difficult to ascertain their origins, thus there has been no intention to breach anybody's copyright. Special thanks go to photographers: Eddie Whitham, who has unearthed some wonderful pictures from his archives; Andrew Varley, top Rugby League photographer and friend since the very early days of the former "Open Rugby" magazine, and another old friend of many years, Andrew Cudbertson. Thanks also to: Andy Wheelwright, Sam Coulter, Ron Bailey, John Etty, Bill Nelson, John Donovan and all friends for their help in providing pictures.

- **6** League Tables - how they finished in 2008.
- **7** Sam Burgess - our front cover boy.
- **8** On the line - the season in review.
- **10** Parkside Thrills - great tries at Hunslet.
- **11** A Century of Great Britain - tribute section.
- **20** All the British international captains.
- **23** Warrington memories in colour.
- **24** Leeds Loyalty - homegrown at Headingley.
- **26** The Golden Boys - who were the world's best.
- **28** Joe Levula's leap - from Fiji to Rochdale.
- **30** The Battens - an amazing family dynasty.
- **32** Sam Obst - from Whitehaven to Wakefield.
- **35** Saints Style - the stars of St.Helens.
- **36** Barrow Flyers - the top wingers of Furness.
- **38** When Rugby League went out on the road.
- **40** Terry Clawson - 23 years at the top.
- **41** Halifax - a battle of two Welsh full-backs.
- **42** Pioneers of Broadcasting.
- **44** Senior Service - Keith's still going strong.
- **45** Club Nostalgia - files on all the old clubs.
- **78** Would you believe it? Funny tales.
- **79** Gregg's schoolboy capers at Whitehaven.
- **80** Jason Robinson - a Wigan world champion .
- **83** Enter the Time Tunnel - the past remembered.
- **94** Catalan Gold - hitting the jackpot in Perpignan.
- **96** The year in Amateur Rugby League.
- **98** The Year in Australia.
- **99** The Year in New Zealand.
- **100** The Year in France.
- **102** New Horizons in 2008.
- **103** Great Britain international players register.
- **110** The other Great Britain international players.
- **111** Did you know? All the Quiz answers.
- **112** The Final Whistle.

This book is dedicated to those who built the spirit of Test football

Another Ashes series over with Great Britain the winners, and the players congratulate each other and exchange friendly greetings in the best spirit of Test match Rugby League. This was in 1962 at the Sydney Cricket Ground as Britain's Alex Murphy and Australia's Mike Cleary shake hands.

Introduction

WELCOME to the fifth edition of this Annual produced by our quarterly magazine *"Rugby League Journal."* In each of those five years we have introduced ourselves the same way, by expressing the wish that our readers will enjoy another huge selection of memorabilia and nostalgia as we remember the Rugby League game we knew in years gone by. Our publication is described as "for fans who don't want to forget," and we know so many of you enjoy re-visiting memories of the players, teams and famous events of the past.

In this Annual we pay special tribute to the story of the Great Britain team as it celebrated its first century. The life and times of the British national team is one thing that binds together people through all generations and from different places; it is a history that we can all share and be fascinated by. All of us were brought up learning the stories about the British teams on tour to Australia, the legends like *"Rorke's Drfit"* and the heroic players who had travelled far from their own small communities to play on what seemed like the vast arena of the Sydney Cricket Ground in front of huge crowds of hostile Aussie supporters. For the Australians, of course, things worked in reverse and their folklore was built around tales of their touring teams enduring the cold of bleak winters in the north of England, old hotels in Ilkley and moments of pure craziness as they journeyed on through France.

Everybody had grown up with the the cycle of tours back and forth to Australia always being set at the same time of year. Great Britain would tour down-under in our summer, whilst the Aussies - or Kiwis - would come to England in the Autumn and then move on to France as winter really set in and Christmas time approached. It was a pattern so many of us set our bodyclocks by, and my biggest regret about the British game's switch to a summer season is that it has destroyed that wonderful tradition of international tours.

Some of you will know that for many years I published a magazine called *"Open Rugby"* and now, of course, the *"Rugby League Journal."* In all the years I've been producing publications about the sport I grew up with, the biggest difficulty has always been trying to get other people to see what I call "the big picture" - tackling the issues that effect the whole game, worldwide, rather than just concentrating on their own little piece of it. With that in mind I always believe it is essential that those people charged with looking after the game's welfare, both now and in the future, must be aware of some of its history - and the realities of the game. That means knowing and having empathy with the people who play it and those who have given so much to support it and maintain it.

In basic terms, I've always been able to divide Rugby League up between two different types of people: those who want to give, and those who only want to take from it. Delving further, that means there are some people who

(Above) Memories of the Great Britain team in action in Australia. This picture is from the 1970 Ashes series first Test bloodbath in Brisbane, as British forwards Dave Robinson and Doug Laughton bring down an Aussie.

can come into the game because it suits their purposes, probably earn a lot of money from it, and then move on to something else. On the other hand, there are people who have given their whole lives to the game, who will still be doing their best for it when those others have taken their salaries and moved on - and who might be left to try and pick up the pieces of the messes created by people who don't really share their passion or understanding.

The rock solid foundations of Rugby League are those volunteers who run the Amateur clubs, and those who contribute so much to keeping their local (semi) professional clubs alive. Sometimes they see a new chairman come into their club, who starts throwing loads of money around to bring in players who have agents doing all they can to increase their fees, and - as if by surprise - it all goes belly up when they realise they've created a huge financial mess. Those who've created the mess move on, just like players and managers in football (and now in Rugby League) - but supporters don't - cannot - change their allegiences. Their club is their club, for life. Just like, for some of us, Rugby League is our game, for life.

No matter what changes affect the game - and let's face it, I never thought I'd see the day when a Challenge Cup Final involving St.Helens was refereed by an official from St.Helens; or a player who was cup-tied could break the rules of eligibility not once, but twice, and still be allowed to go on and play in the Wembley Final in the same year; or that clear forward passes would be accepted as part of the game - Rugby League is the game we still get passionate about. The memories of what brought us to the game all those many years ago will always remain - and I hope you can enjoy sharing some of those memories in this Annual and in our future quarterly editions of *"Rugby League Journal."* Happy reading.

Harry Edgar (Editor)

HOW THEY FINISHED
FINAL LEAGUE TABLES 2008

SUPER LEAGUE

	P	W	D	L	For	Ag.	Diff	Pts
St. Helens	27	21	1	5	940	457	483	43
Leeds	27	21	0	6	863	413	450	42
Catalans	27	16	2	9	694	625	69	34
Wigan	27	13	3	11	648	698	-50	29
Bradford	27	14	0	13	705	625	80	28
Warrington	27	14	0	13	690	713	-23	28
Hull K.R.	27	11	1	15	564	713	-149	23
Wakefield Trin.	27	11	0	16	574	760	-186	22
Harlequins	27	11	0	16	569	763	-194	22
Huddersfield	27	10	1	16	638	681	-43	21
Hull	27	8	1	18	538	699	-161	17
Castleford	27	7	1	19	593	869	-276	15

NATIONAL LEAGUE ONE

	P	W	D	L	Bonus	For	Ag.	Pts
Salford	18	12	3	3	3	614	302	45
Celtic Crus.	18	12	0	6	4	511	391	40
Halifax	18	11	1	6	3	634	514	38
Leigh	18	10	0	8	4	448	448	34
Whitehaven	18	10	0	8	2	420	399	32
Widnes**	18	10	2	6	5	453	410	30
Sheffield	18	8	1	9	3	425	530	29
Featherstone	18	6	1	11	6	452	515	26
Batley	18	5	0	13	8	387	538	23
Dewsbury	18	2	0	16	7	315	612	13

(**Nine points deducted for entering administration)

NATIONAL LEAGUE TWO

	P	W	D	L	Bonus	For	Ag.	Pts
Gateshead	22	19	0	3	2	767	415	59
Barrow	22	16	0	6	4	703	375	52
Oldham	22	17	0	5	1	716	456	52
Doncaster	22	15	0	7	3	672	426	48
Keighley	22	15	0	7	3	611	519	48
York	22	11	1	10	7	740	540	42
Rochdale	22	10	1	11	4	715	610	36
Workington	22	6	0	16	10	512	628	28
Blackpool	22	7	1	14	2	472	828	25
Swinton	22	6	0	16	4	482	777	22
London Skol.	22	4	1	17	6	449	823	20
Hunslet	22	4	0	18	5	336	778	17

ROBBIE PAUL - enjoyed a succesful year with Salford.

DREAM TEAMS

The official "All Star" selections for the 2008 season named by the Rugby Football League in conjunction with their media associates - *not* this publication.

SUPER LEAGUE

1-Clint Greenshields (Catalans); **2-Scott Donald** (Leeds), **3-Matt Gidley** (St.Helens), **4-George Carmont** (Wigan), **5-Ade Gardner** (St.Helens); **6-Leon Pryce** (St.Helens), **7-Rob Burrow** (Leeds); **8-James Graham** (St.Helens), **9-Keiron Cunningham** (St.Helens), **10-Jamie Peacock** (Leeds), **11-Gareth Ellis** (Leeds), **12-Ben Westwood** (Warrington), **13-Kevin Sinfield** (Leeds).

NATIONAL LEAGUE ONE

1-Tony Duggan (Celtic Crusaders); **2-Dean Gaskell** (Widnes), **3-Mark Dalle-Court** (Celtic Crusaders), **4-John Wilshere** (Salford), **5-Paul White** (Salford); **6-Damien Quinn** (Celtic Crusaders), **7-Richard Myler** (Salford); **8-Craig Stapleton** (Salford), **9-Sean Penkywicz** (Halifax), **10-Philip Leuluai** (Salford), **11-Lee Doran** (Leigh), **12-Darren Mapp** (Celtic Crusaders), **13-Neale Wyatt** (Celtic Crusaders).

NATIONAL LEAGUE TWO

1-Paul O'Connor (Oldham); **2-Stewart Sanderson** (Gateshead), **3-Marcus St.Hilaire** (Oldham), **4-Ben McAlpine** (Gateshead), **5-James Nixon** (Barrow); **6-Kyle Briggs** (Doncaster), **7-Dan Russell** (Gateshead); **8-Andy Shickell** (Keighley), **9-Corey Lawrie** (Doncaster), **10-Richard Mervill** (Oldham), **11-Michael Knowles** (Gateshead), **12-Danny Halliwell** (Oldham), **13-Dave Armistead** (Barrow).

THE 2009 ANNUAL'S FRONT COVER STAR - SAM BURGESS

CARRYING RUGBY LEAGUE'S GREAT TRADITION

Photo by ANDREW VARLEY

SAM BURGESS in action in his international debut for Great Britain against New Zealand in the 2007 Test series.

We are proud to have Sam Burgess adorn the front cover of this *"Rugby League Journal Annual 2009"* - pictured in action for Great Britain in their last home Test series versus New Zealand. Sam, we believe, is a symbol of all that is good about Rugby League Football, bearing the qualities that the game has embodied since its very birth.

Through the many different ages, different rules and different styles of play, some things in Rugby League have not - can not - change. The understated toughness, the natural skills, the sportsmanship and the unspoken realism and humbleness of its players, has endured through all the generations. Sam Burgess, of Bradford, England and Great Britain, continues that fine tradition. He comes from a family with great sporting background: Sam's brother Luke plays for Leeds and his younger twin brothers have now joined him at the Bradford Bulls.

The strength of Sam's performances for Bradford won him a rapid elevation to Test status in 2007; he continued his international progress by representing England in France during the summer of 2008, and it was a big blow to his country's hopes when injury ruled him out of the World Cup. All this has seen Sam Burgess carry on one of Rugby League's great traditions - that of the teenage prodigy. His impressive size and physical strength for a lad of his age enabled him to break into first team football at just 17-years-of-age, but the Burgess determination and maturity ensured he could go further and make the progression to Test football without any fuss. In 2008, in a Bradford side badly hit by injuries, Sam Burgess stepped up to the plate, took on extra responsibilities and showed his leadership qualities.

All this has happened whilst still a teenager. Burgess made his Great Britain debut aged just 18, once again underlining the famed Rugby League motto of: *"If they're good enough, they're old enough."* In doing so, Sam was following in some very famous footsteps, as so many of the game's greatest players were teenage internationals. None greater than the legendary Harold Wagstaff, who made his first team debut for Huddersfield aged just 15 years and 175 days; and his England bow at just 17 years and 228 days (making him still the youngest England international of all time.) Billy Batten, before Wagstaff, had made his Test debut whilst still in his teens and, throughout the history of the game, the tradition has been maintained - two of our finest half-backs Alex Murphy and Roger Millward, were just turned 19 and 18 respectively when they first played for Great Britain; Neil Fox was ony 16 when he debuted for Wakefield Trinity; Bob Irving was starring as a second-rower in the Ashes Tests of 1967 when barely 18; and in more modern times Shaun Edwards, Paul Newlove and Andy Farrell were also only 18 when they made their Test debuts. Just like Sam Burgess, bringing all Rugby League's finest old qualities to the present day.

PUTTING IT ON THE LINE - THE 2008 SEASON IN REVIEW

No change at the top of British Rugby League in 2008 as both Leeds and St.Helens maintained their grip on the trophies they had locked away twelve months earlier. And there was a remarkable similarity about the way events unfolded just the same as they had in 2007. St.Helens won the Challenge Cup, clinched the League Leaders' shield, and went into the Super League Grand Final again as hot favourites - only to be denied for a second year running by a Leeds side who definitely saved their best 'till last.

Saints' dreams of sending their departing coach Daniel Anderson on his way with a Cup and Championship "double" to celebrate, were washed away in the torrential rain that marred the Old Trafford showpiece on the first Saturday of October. Leeds didn't sweep St.Helens aside with the same razzle-dazzle football they had produced in the previous year's Grand Final, in 2008 they steadily ground Saints down in an intensely physical battle up-front and then issued the knockout blows with tremendous pieces of skilful opportunism.

Leeds magnificent Grand Final

It was a magnificent Grand Final performance by Leeds, winning 24 points to 16 in a contest they entered as underdogs to a St.Helens side who had dominated the season and won 23 consecutive victories. Nobody was better than young Lee Smith, switched to full-back as a late replacement for the injured Brent Webb, and producing the performance of his life to win the coveted Harry Sunderland Trophy - presented in memory of one of Rugby League's greatest publicists.

Before that night at Old Trafford, everything seemed to be going to script for St.Helens in 2008, with Daniel Anderson set to bow out a winner after a tremendously positive three years at Knowsley Road. Week in, week out, Saints were the best team in the Super League competition, and they had the outstanding individuals in such as Paul Wellens, Leon Pryce, Shaun Long, James Graham and the evergreen Keiron Cunningham. Prop-forward Graham was voted by his peers the "Man of Steel" as the Super League's player of the year for 2008. He said he was embarrassed to be nominated ahead of such a great player as Cunningham, but the young Liverpudlian with Cumbrian roots really came of age in

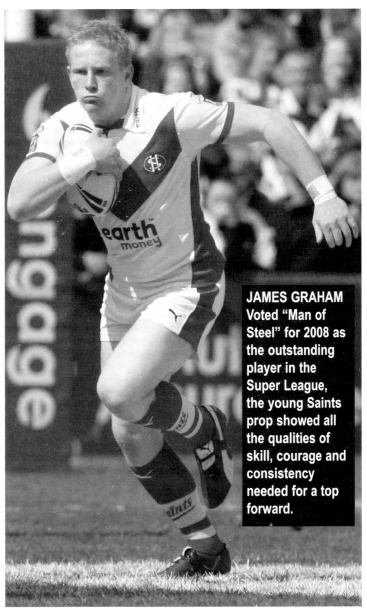

JAMES GRAHAM Voted "Man of Steel" for 2008 as the outstanding player in the Super League, the young Saints prop showed all the qualities of skill, courage and consistency needed for a top forward.

2008 - getting far more game time on the field, he revelled in it and got the opportunity to produce the handling skills and physicality that were a throwback to the great prop-forwards of the past.

St.Helens won the Challenge Cup for the third year in a row, going back to the new Wembley to defeat Hull in the Final on the last Saturday in August. Pre-match predictions had Saints as such clear favourites, there were fears the showpiece Final could result in one of those awful blowout scorelines the game sees too often these days. Happily, the fears were unfounded as Hull rose to the occasion and gave Saints a run for their money before eventually going down 28-16 in front of an attendance officially given as 82,821. This year's Challenge Cup competition had earlier broken new ground when the semi-final between Hull and Wakefield was staged at Doncaster's Keepmoat Stadium. At that time there were very realistic hopes that the 2008 Challenge Cup Final would be a repeat of the infamous "Watersplash Final" of forty years earlier, between Leeds and Wakefield Trinity - but, it was not to be, and the occasion was tinged with sadness by the death, shortly before the Final, of Don Fox - who had been such a pivotal figure in that game in 1968.

With Leeds and St.Helens dominating again, there's no doubt that Super League's most exciting story in 2008 was the successful rise of the Catalan Dragons. The French club achieved third place in the League - something way beyond their wildest dreams when they first entered the competition just three seasons ago. Their major *raison d'etre* was to try to revitalise public interest and the playing fortunes of the game in France, but looked at purely from the Super League's point of view there's no doubt that the Dragons have breathed a new excitement into the competition. As well as offering English club supporters the chance to have an overseas trip to follow their teams in Perpignan, they have the novelty of being very "different." The significant point is that the Catalans' success has been achieved without any British input at all to their playing and coaching staff - all are either native Frenchmen or Australasian imports. Their success in 2008 was achieved despite learning, early in the season, that their coach Mick Potter would be leaving to take over from Daniel Anderson at St.Helens next year. That did not stop Potter achieving the "Coach of the Year" accolade, and here is a man who will certainly be experiencing a change in lifestyle once he moves to his new post.

(Above) LEE SMITH the young Leeds star of the 2008 Grand Final and winner of the coveted Harry Sunderland award for man of the match as the Rhinos retained their Championship title.

(Left) Another side of the world of Super League in 2008 - Wakefield's official match programme without any reference to the proud name of Trinity.

Salford the winners and bravo Gateshead

Much attention in 2008 was focussed on the Rugby Football League's decision to expand the Super League from next year and bring an additional two clubs into the competition under the new "licencing" system. It was no big surprise that Salford and the Celtic Crusaders were the chosen two and, as both operated with squads of full-time professionals, it was also no surprise that they should finish in the top two places in National League One and eventually qualify for the Grand Final - although neither were truly dominant over other teams like Halifax, Widnes and Whitehaven. In that decider played at Warrington, the Celtic side from Bridgend were desperately unlucky not to carry off the title. In the end, it took one last penalty decision for Salford just seconds from the end of normal time which the Reds were able to convert to force a draw and extra-time. Having got out of gaol, Salford made no mistake and clinched the National League One championship to go with their League Leaders' trophy and the Northern Rail Cup, which they won in a Final at Blackpool against the surprise packets from Doncaster.

The Dons must have thought major Finals like buses - having waited all their life since 1951 to get to one, within a few weeks they'd got to another - the second time they made no mistake, beating Oldham in the National League Two play-off to clinch the third promotion spot behind Gateshead and Barrow. The success of Gateshead really did warm the hearts of those who have seen their struggles to keep their club alive on tiny crowds over the past few years - so it was bravo to their coach, Dave Woods, and especially to all the local North East lads in their team who have flown the flag for Rugby League in this outpost against all the odds. The National Leagues, once again, provided close competitions full of excitement and entertainment - all worthy of far bigger audiences.

FLYING TRIES AT THE OLD HUNSLET GROUND

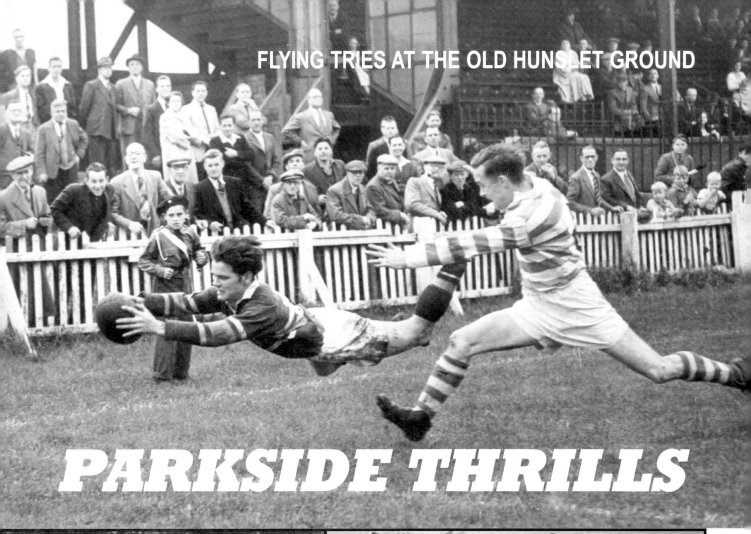

PARKSIDE THRILLS

Geoff Gunney, the man who gave everything to the life of Hunslet, pictured touching down for a try at his beloved Parkside fifty years ago in 1958. The opponents were Huddersfield and in support of Geoff is Hunslet's winger Garside.

The old Hunslet ground at Parkside closed its doors in 1973 and so ended not just a chapter, but a whole volume, in the history of Rugby League. Thanks largely to Geoff Gunney, a new page was turned and a new Hunslet club continued - as they do to this day - but for those who can remember Parkside in the happy days before it started to fall into disrepair, nothing can match the vision of a packed crowd *"Sweeping the Seas"* as they roared Hunslet home. The team in the distinctive myrtle, white and flame jerseys created plenty of spectacular action for photographers at Parkside. The picture at the top was a famous one which adorned the front cover of the *"Parksider"* programme for several years, it shows Hunslet winger Tate diving over to score against Batley in 1956. Below that, we see Huddersfield's Lionel Cooper in another spectacular dive to score against Hunslet in a Yorkshire Cup tie.

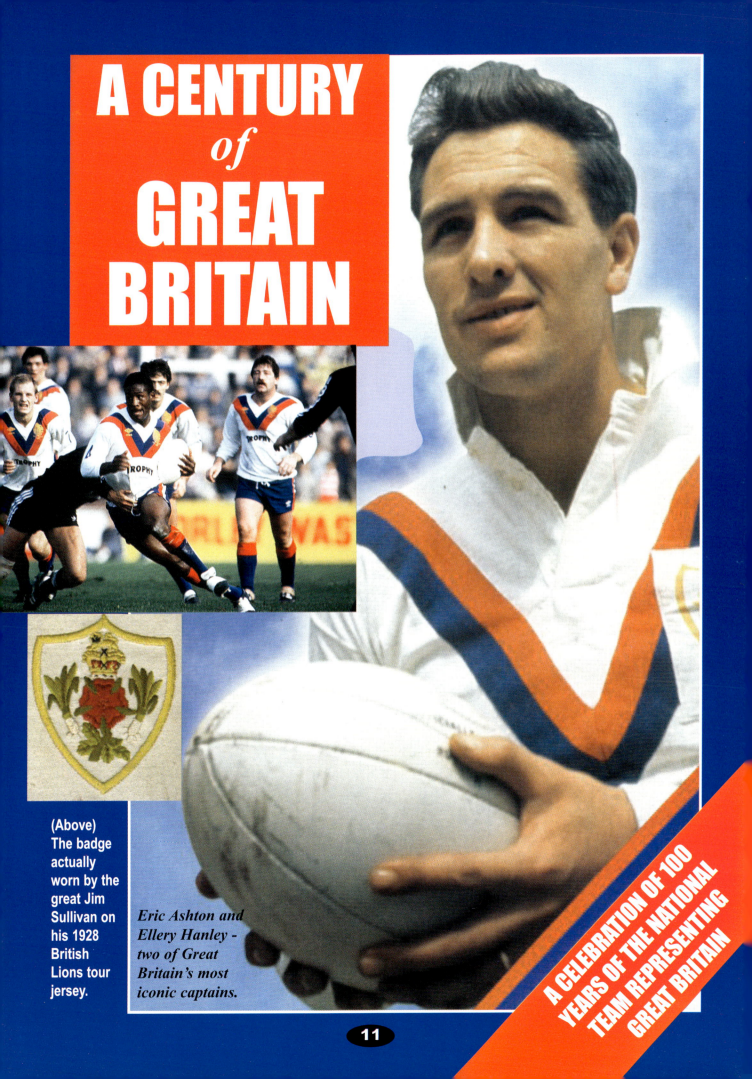

A CENTURY of GREAT BRITAIN

(Above) The badge actually worn by the great Jim Sullivan on his 1928 British Lions tour jersey.

Eric Ashton and Ellery Hanley - two of Great Britain's most iconic captains.

A CELEBRATION OF 100 YEARS OF THE NATIONAL TEAM REPRESENTING GREAT BRITAIN

A CENTURY of GREAT BRITAIN

TAKE A LOOK BACK

LEON PRYCE, one of the modern day stars of the last Great Britain team in 2007, looks back over his shoulder at some of the great memories from the British team in the past.

Jonathan Davies

Clive Sullivan

Shaun Edwards

Photo by
ANDREW VARLEY PICTURE AGENCY

A CENTURY of GREAT BRITAIN

100 years of being the best of the British nation

Just eight years after the formation of the Northern Union, the honourable men who had been brave enough to stand up for what they believed in and "go it alone," found themselves able to take a giant leap forward in cementing the future of their new game. This came about thanks to the arrival of the first New Zealand touring team in 1907 inspired by the visionary young pioneer from Wellington, Albert Baskerville.

By the first month of the year 1908, the time was ready for a team to be selected to represent the very best of the Northern Union in three matches against the touring New Zealanders - and so the very first Test match, and the first Test series, was played. Harry Taylor, the team's full-back from Hull, captained the first British international team as they kicked off their brave new world at Headingley on the Saturday afternoon of 25th January, 1908. And Taylor's side got things off to a winning start with a 14-6 victory over the New Zealanders.

Following the success of the tour by Baskerville's so-called "All Golds," less than a year later the Northern Union were playing host to another team from the colonies, this one brought from Australia by another brave entrepreneur, James Giltinan. These were the first Kangaroos, and so began Rugby League's greatest international rivalry which would come to be known as the battle for the Ashes, between Great Britain and Australia.

Recognising the enormous boost to the game given by the provision of genuine international football, the Northern Union wasted little time in embarking on its own first overseas tour when, in 1910, the inaugral Lions touring team set out on the high seas for Australasia. Captained by James "Jumbo" Lomas - a Salford player at the time but a native of Maryport in Cumberland - this first Lions team thus began one of our sports most symbolic institutions, with future generations of players all regarding selection for a Lions tour as the ultimate honour the game could offer. And, in the decades that were to follow Lomas and his men of 1910, the Test series in Australia were also to become highly profitable financially for the British Rugby League.

So, in less than three years following the arrival of young Baskerville and his first New Zealand touring team, the foundations had been set in stone for the invigorating future of the team representing Great Britain - with the four-yearly cycle of tours back and forth to Australia interrupted only by the dark days of two World Wars.

Although the Aussies would invariably refer to the British team simply as "England," the official title of Northern Union was maintained for our team all the way through to 1922, when the pressure of its burgeoning international strength gave rise to the name of the game in its country of birth being changed to "Rugby League." Thus, the first time we played Test matches under the title

A reminder of the fine contribution made to the British team by men from all nations of the United Kingdom as *(above)* we see Welshman John Thorley and Scotsman David Rose in action in Great Britain's first ever World Cup match, against Australia in Lyon's *Stade de Gerland* in 1954.

of England came on the 1924 Lions tour - and the name England was maintained until 1947 despite the fact that the team invariably contained players from Wales. In total, over 100 Welshmen have played in Test Rugby League and nine of them captained the British side. During the time our team was called England, two of its greatest captains were Welshmen, Jim Sullivan and Gus Risman. Two Scotsmen, Dave Valentine and George Fairbairn, have also captained Great Britain.

The title of "Great Britain" was first used in the 1947 home series against New Zealand, and that's the way it has stayed ever since - and the way almost all surviving generations have grown up with as the name of Rugby League's national team. In the 1950s, Great Britain's activity was increased with the launch of the World Cup and the decision to grant full Test status to games against France. But now, in their wisdom, the current rulers of the Rugby Football League - some possibly haven't even heard of great men in the story of the international game, like Baskerville, Giltinan, Lomas, Sullivan, Risman, or John Wilson - decreed that from here on, there will be no more British team. Instead, any future Test matches will be contested by an England team containing, naturally enough, just Englishmen. That meant the British team played on home soil for the last time against New Zealand in 2007 - and the century of Great Britain was complete.

A CENTURY of GREAT BRITAIN

Wagstaff's 1914 Lions, the second Northern Union touring team to visit Australia, pictured in action in Sydney.

Building the legends of the international game

As in most sports, the international stage was where all the greatest legends of the Rugby League game were built. And, in the case of the British team, the majority were developed far away on the fields of Australia rather than home soil. The dramas were encouraged, of course, by the romance of being so far away on the other side of the world and the sheer magnitude of playing before such huge crowds on the Sydney Cricket Ground, far bigger than anything generated for international games back in Britain.

To this day, the greatest legend remains the exploit of the British team captained by Harold Wagstaff in 1914, in which they won a deciding Test in Sydney against such overwhelming odds that their epic struggle has gone down in the annals of the game as *"Rorke's Drift."* For years afterwards, the 13 players who "did their duty" for their country that day would have the initials *"R.D."* printed beside their names in the list of Test appearances in the Rugby Football League's "Official Guide."

Harold Wagstaff is a name revered in Rugby League history and no captain was more popular. Some six years after *"Rorke's Drift"* and after the ravages of the Great War had taken their toll, including three members of Wagstaff's 1914 touring team, the great Yorkshireman bade farewell to international rugby in the final Test of the 1921-22 Ashes series played at Salford. Playing against Australia for the last time under the title of the "Northern Union," Wagstaff's team regained the Ashes and the skipper was carried shoulder high from the Weaste field by delighted supporters.

By this time another future British captain had entered the fray and he, too, was destined to become a legend of the game. His name was Jonty Parkin, a scrum-half from Wakefield, and he was an inspirational leader of both the 1924 and 1928 Lions touring teams which came home with the Ashes. In the decisive Test of the 1928 series, Parkin played on with a broken thumb in quagmire conditions in Sydney. Both Harold Wagstaff and Jonty Parkin were automatic first choices for the "Hall of Fame."

The last time the team was called the Northern Union before changing to "England" was in the 1921-22 Ashes series played at home. This is the team which won the opening Test 6-5 at Headingley in October, 1921, and includes two of the greatest early legends of the game - Harold Wagstaff and Jonty Parkin. The picture shows, left to right: *(Standing):* Arthur Johnson (Widnes) reserve, Billy Cunliffe (Warrington), Joe Cartwright (Leigh), Edgar Morgan (Hull), Jack Price (Broughton R.), Jack Beames (Halifax), George Skelhorne (Warrington), Mr.S.Foster (manager). *(Seated):* Billy Stone (Hull), Gwyn Thomas (Huddersfield), Harold Wagstaff (Huddersfield) captain, Jim Bacon (Leeds), Squire Stockwell (Leeds). *(In front):* Johnny Rogers (Huddersfield), Jonty Parkin (Wakefield).

A CENTURY of GREAT BRITAIN

Britain dominated the Ashes

The 1932 Lions in action in Australia as hooker Les White (of Hunslet) drives his way through the defence of the Sydney Metropolitan team and dives over for the first try of the tour. The other British players in support include the Swinton greats, Bryn Evans (vice-captain of the 1932 touring team) and mighty Cumbrian forward Martin Hodgson.

Great Britain's most conclusive era of dominance of the international game came in the years between the two World Wars. In fact, the Australians endured an Ashes drought which was to last for 30 years, never in anybody's wildest dreams (or nightmares!) imagining that one day the boot would be on the other foot and it would be the British not having won the Ashes for fully 38 years - and counting ...

Australia won the Ashes in the 1920 series, and did not regain them until 1950 - in between some of the greatest stories of British Rugby League folklore were written and some of its most imposing players strode the international stage. Jonty Parkin became the first man to make three Lions tours, the last two as captain in 1924 and 1928, and he was succeded as the skipper by the great Welsh full-back Jim Sullivan. "Big Jim" was like a colussus at the back for the British side, his goal-kicking winning many Test matches - but one wonders how he, and the numerous other outstanding Welsh players, really felt about being described as "English" wherever they played. There would be no such questions asked about the other stars of this era like: Alf Ellaby and Stanley Smith - the flying wingers; centres like Stan Brogden and the powerful Arthur Atkinson; and mighty forwards (who were giants for their time) like Nat Silcock, Jack Arkwright, Martin Hodgson and Harry Beverley. Sullivan was unable to make a third tour in 1936 and the captaincy moved on to the Cumbrian Jim Brough, as another all-time great British leader began to emerge in the shape of Gus Risman (another Welshman.) Gus would have captained the 1940 Lions had the War not caused it to be abandoned, but he achieved his destiny six years later as the captain of the famous 1946 *"Indomitables"* - the touring team who travelled to Australia on an aircrfat carrier and became the only British team to return undefeated from a three-match Ashes series. Risman's *"Indomitables"* were the last British side to be called England, as by the time the 1947 Kiwis arrived, we had finally become "Great Britain."

A CENTURY of GREAT BRITAIN

Players wore their national colours with pride

The very first poinst scored by a British player in Test football was a drop-goal by half-back Jim Jolley (of Runcorn) in the first match of the series against the "All Golds" at Leeds on 25th January, 1908.

The very last points came in the shape of a penalty-goal kicked by another half-back, Rob Burrow (of Leeds) also against New Zealand, this time on 10th November, 2007 at Wigan - in what we are led to believe will be Great Britain's last ever Test match on their home soil.

The first British Test try was scored by winger Jim Leytham (of Wigan) in that same first match in 1908, and the last British Test try was scored by stand-off Danny McGuire (of Leeds) in that same last match in 2007. Fittingly, McGuire's try was a very, very good one, worthy of the memory of all the great British tries of the previous 100 years and - a real rarity in the modern game - was created from a planned move involving a kick direct from a scrum.

Playing for Great Britain has always brought the best out of talented players, and some of their famous Test match tries will always stand up in any era as being truly great. Certainly for those fans today who are lucky enough to possess videos or DVDs showing film of famous Test matches from the past, they will never grow tired of watching some of the magical tries created by Great Britain players.

A try by winger Johnny Lawrenson as Great Britain wrapped up the Ashes against Australia at Station Road, Swinton in October, 1948.

A brief cameo of these would include such as:

Ike Southward - tearing down the wing from Alex Murphy's break in the famous Brisbane Test of 1958.

Mick Sullivan - completing a 100 yard try by collecting Eric Fraser's kick ahead in the third 1958 Test in Sydney.

Alex Murphy - going over 40 yards like a bullet direct from a scrum in the third Test in 1962 at the S.C.G.

Don Fox - completing a marvellous move of inter-passing against the Aussies at Headingley in a 1963 bloodbath.

Chris Young - the winger from Hull K.R. showing great pace and power to outflank the Australian defence down the South Stand side at Headingley in the 1967 first Test.

Dennis Hartley - the big prop charging down a kick and sprinting to the line in the 1970 Ashes decider in Sydney.

Clive Sullivan - an unforgettable run of over 75 yards down the touchline in the 1972 World Cup Final in Lyon.

Garry Schofield - a brilliant try under the posts at the Sydney Cricket Ground fom Des Drummond's explosive run and one handed pass in the first Ashes Test in 1984 ; followed by an even better one from the 18-year-old Schofield as he finished an incredible length-of-the-field combined move in the second Test at Brisbane.

Joe Lydon - supported the brilliant Ellery Hanley to finish an 80-yard moved in front of the main stand at Headingley against New Zealand in 1985.

Mike Gregory - took Andy Gregory's pass and outpaced the Aussie defence for over 70 yards to seal a victory in Sydney in 1988.

Martin Offiah - goose-stepping to the line after turning the New Zealand defence inside-out at Old Trafford in the first Test in 1989.

Jonathan Davies - arching around the Australian defence on a 60 yard run to score in a great win at Wembley in the 1994 Ashes.

Alex Murphy - one of Britain's greatest ever players - pictured in action in the last of his 27 internationals, the second Test of the 1971 series versus New Zealand. With a crowd of only 4,000 present at Castleford that day, and Britain losing a home series to the Kiwis for the first time since the "All Golds" in 1908, it was all a far cry for Alex compared to his glory days in Australia in 1958 and 1962. The other British players in the forefront of the picture are Tony Karalius (on the floor) Colin Dixon and Bob Haigh. The referee is Deryck Brown.

A CENTURY of GREAT BRITAIN

Here come the Ashes ... for the last time. This was the moment, on 4th July, 1970, when Great Britain were about to seal their victory before the packed hill at the Sydney Cricket Ground. Doug Laughton has broken through the Australian defence and a split second later gave the pass to the supporting Roger Millward which sent the mercurial stand-off scampering away for Britain's fifth and clinching try. Great Britain won this third Test 21-17 and with it the Ashes.

Remembering glory days

After the British dominance of the game in the years before and immediately after World War Two, things changed in Rugby League in the second half of the 20th Century and beyond. In that time, Great Britain still enjoyed many glory days ... can you remember these?

* **Valentine's World Cup heroes** - when Scotsman Dave Valentine led a team of British "no hopers" to victory in the first World Cup, played in France in 1954.
* **Prescott's Epic** - as skipper and prop-forward Alan Prescott played all but four minutes of the decisive Brisbane Test in 1958 with a broken arm to inspire his injury-hit team to a vitally needed victory.
* **Ashton and his team of greats** - the 1962 Great Britain touring team swept the Aussies aside to win the Ashes, thanks to the class of great players like Alex Murphy, Mick Sullivan, Brian McTigue and Dick Huddart.
* **Myler's Ashes winners** - Frank Myler captained the 1970 Lions to Ashes victory in Sydney and nobody could have guessed we'd still be waiting for a repeat.

(Above) Malcolm Reilly in the winning 1970 Ashes series.

* **Sullivan's World Cup magic** - another World Cup triumph in France, helped by a magical Clive Sullivan try.
* **Schofield's try quartet** - four tries by Garry Schofield inspired a vital 1985 win against the Kiwis at Wigan.
* **Hanley's Wembley masterpiece** - a huge Wembley crowd in 1990 saw Ellery's greatest Test performance.

A CENTURY of GREAT BRITAIN

New fields of Test competition for the British team

Although France had arrived on the Rugby League scene in 1934, the British teams' opponents in official Test matches remained restricted to those against the Commonwealth cousins of Australia and New Zealand until the mid-1950s. By then, France's spectacular success in the game, most especially on their inaugural tour to Australia in 1951, meant the French had to be accepted as guests at the top table. The first officially recognised match between Great Britain and France took place in Toulouse in November, 1954 during the first World Cup tournament. It ended in a 13-all draw and brought the kind of frenzy, colour and excitable crowd that British newspaper correspondents had never witnessed before in international Rugby League. It was the first international to be staged in the Toulouse stadium, and the crowd of 37,471 remains the biggest ever for a Rugby League match in France. The two teams met again six days later in Paris to contest the World Cup Final, won by Great Britain 16-12.

Despite the huge success and high entertainment value of those two World Cup games against France, the British Rugby League still would not give Test status to the French until 1957 - that meant five other games between Great Britain and France in the mid-1950s were not officially recognised and the British players who took part in them were denied Test status. The first official Test match against France was staged at Headingley on 26th January,

Geoff Gunney of Hunslet dives over to score a try for Great Britain in their first officially recognised Test match against France - at Headingley in January, 1957.

1957, and a crowd of 20,221 saw Great Britain romp to an easy 45-12 victory. But, just five weeks later, the same two teams drew 19-all back in Toulouse in the first of what were to become familiar examples of how much a local referee, and the motivation of playing at home, could make the French look like a totally different team. It was a pattern that was to be repeated many times over the following thirty years, with Anglo-French encounters rarely without controversy. Sometimes, the violent clashes and refereeing problems would boil over completely, and ugly scenes would provoke various British officials over the years to claim we should stop playing in France. One of the most notorious incidents came at Swinton in 1965, when the French captain Marcel Bescos was sent off by referee Dennis Davies but refused to leave the field - prompting Mr.Davies to walk off and temporarily abandon the game.

A fourth Test match opponent for Great Britain appeared in 1984 when they played Papua New Guinea for the first time - the British team, captained by Brian Noble, winning 38-20 in Mount Hagan, playing in surroundings and conditions that the founding fathers of the Northern Union could never have envisaged when they took their first steps into Test match football at Headingley in 1908. By then, Papua New Guinea were long-standing members of the International Board and Rugby League was their national game - but a much more unlikely fifth opponent were Fiji, whom Great Britain played for the only time on their ill-fated "Super League" tour of 1996. And, in an indication of the way fantasy was about to overtake reality in many areas of Rugby League, Britain won this Test match 72-4.

Andy Gregory scores for Great Britain in their first home Test versus Papua New Guinea, at Central Park, Wigan in 1987.

A CENTURY of GREAT BRITAIN

The Great Britain team pictured at St.Helens on Wednesday 10th April, 1957, before going out to beat France by 29-14. The players are, left to right: *(Standing):* Johnny Whiteley (Hull - reserve forward), Phil Jackson (Barrow), Derek Turner (Oldham), Sid Little (Oldham), Billy Boston (Wigan), Mick Sullivan (Huddersfield), Lewis Jones (Leeds), Geoff Gunney (Hunslet), Austin Rhodes (St.Helens - reserve back). *(In front):* Ray Price (Warrington), Jeff Stevenson (Leeds), Alan Prescott (St.Helens - captain), Glyn Moses (St.Helens), Tommy Harris (Hull) and Jack Grundy (Barrow). A crowd of 23,250 at Knowsley Road paid receipts of £2,650 to watch this Test match refereed by Mr. Matt Coates of Pudsey.

Don't forget the boys selected in the Shadow Team

In years gone by when Great Britain regularly played several Test matches during the course of each season, there was always much space devoted in the press to speculation over team selection, just as there continues to be in other major team sports now.

And Rugby League always added an extra dimension to that interest by publicly naming the so-called "Shadow Team" - effectively reserves on stand-by, a full team of them covering every position from one to thirteen, ready to step into the full international team should any of the first XIII become unavailable due to injury or other unforseen circumstances.

Many very fine players in the Rugby League never got to play for their country, but were still able to enjoy an added status by being described as "Great Britain Shadow" players. As an example of this, we refer to a directive (they weren't called Press Releases in the days when Bill Fallowfield was at the helm) issued from the Rugby Football League at Chapeltown Road in Leeds in late October, 1957 which some newspapers and club programmes headed *"Our Test Match Team."* It stated:

The team to represent Great Britain against France at Toulouse on Sunday, November 3rd will be:
Bernard Ganley (Oldham); **Billy Boston** (Wigan), **Phil Jackson** (Barrow), **Alan Davies** (Oldham), **Mike Sullivan** (Wigan); **Dave Bolton** (Wigan), **Jeff Stevenson** (Leeds); **Alan Prescott** (St.Helens) *captain,* **Tommy Harris** (Hull), **Ken Jackson** (Oldham), **Dennis Goodwin** (Barrow), **Sid Little** (Oldham), **Derek Turner** (Oldham). *Reserves to travel:* **George Parkinson** (Swinton) and **John Whiteley** (Hull).

Shadow team:
Frank Dyson (Huddersfield); **Bill Smith** (Whitehaven), **Eric Ashton** (Wigan), **Denzil Webster** (York), **Johnny Freeman** (Halifax); **George Parkinson** (Swinton), **Frank Pitchford** (Oldham); **Stan Owen** (Leigh), **John Shaw** (Wakefield Trinity), **Brian McTigue** (Wigan), **John Whiteley** (Hull), **Colin Clift** (Halifax) and **Geoff Robinson** (Whitehaven).

That Great Britain team did play as selected in Toulouse and beat France 25-14.

(Above) **Alan Davies scores a try by the corner-flag in the Test win at Toulouse on 3rd November, as Mick Sulivan looks on.**

A CENTURY of GREAT BRITAIN
THE CAPTAINS

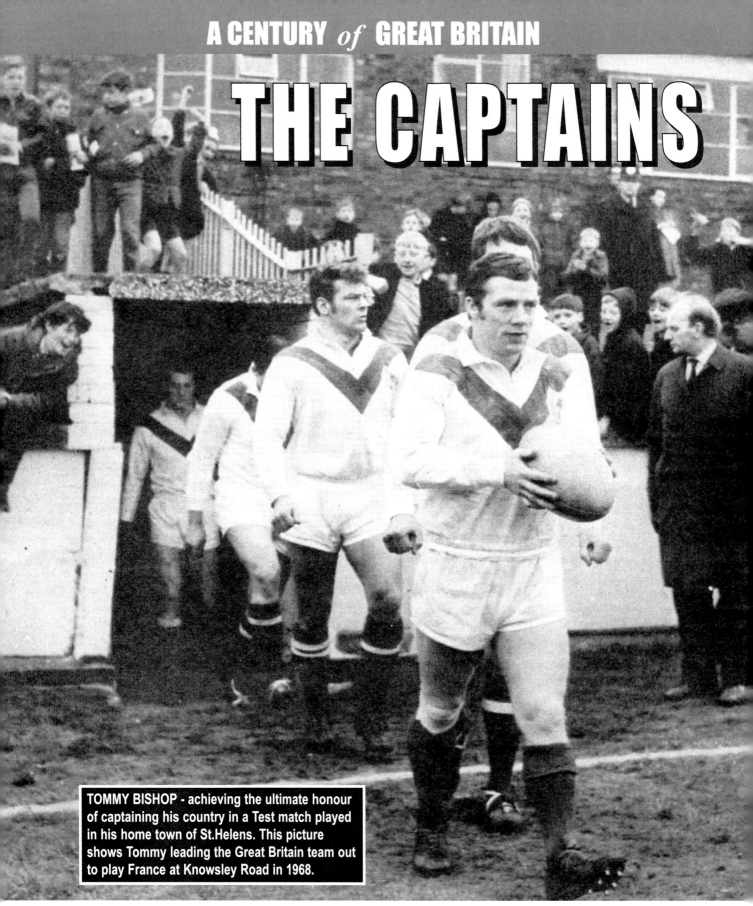

TOMMY BISHOP - achieving the ultimate honour of captaining his country in a Test match played in his home town of St.Helens. This picture shows Tommy leading the Great Britain team out to play France at Knowsley Road in 1968.

To captain the Great Britain team has always been the ultimate honour for any Rugby League player in the U.K., and in the 100 year history of the international team no less than 67 men achieved that honour.

From Harry Taylor in 1908 to Jamie Peacock in 2007, every one of those 67 British players has felt the same pride in being asked to captain their country. Some have come to be elevated to legendary status within the history of the game, most notably such as: James "Jumbo" Lomas the skipper of the very first Lions touring team; Harold Wagstaff, Jonty Parkin and Jim Sullivan from pre-War years and later Gus Risman, Ernest Ward and Eric Ashton.

A CENTURY of GREAT BRITAIN

Within that elite group, others like Alan Prescott and Dave Valentine, have become pivotal figures in the game's folklore for their role as Great Britain captain in specific individual events, rather than an acknowledgement of their whole careers in the Great Britain team.

Sadly for Andrew Farrell, who stands alone as the man to have skippered Great Britain more than any other, he has not come to enjoy that same epic status because, unfortunately for him, all of his 26 captain's knocks came during the "Super League" era when summer rugby reduced the credibility of the international game so much. That meant Farrell never got the chance his talents deserved to lead a full Lions tour to Australia, nor did any of his Great Britain teams manage to win a series against the Australians or, more often than not, New Zealand.

Andrew Farrell also holds the distinction of being the youngest man to captain Great Britain in a Test match - a feat he achieved at the age of 21 years and 121 days against Papua New Guinea at Lae on 28th September, 1996. On the other side of the coin, Britain's oldest Test captain remains the great Gus Risman, who was 35 years and 119 days old when he led the team which became the only Lions side to remain unbeaten in all three Tests of an Ashes series on Australian soil, at the Sydney Cricket Ground on 20th July, 1946.

(Above) JEFF STEVENSON leading the way for Great Britain against France in 1960. Stevenson still stands as the last British captain to lift the Ashes trophy on home soil, a feat he achieved in the 1959 series.

THE GREAT BRITAIN CAPTAINS' ROLL OF HONOUR

- 26 - Andrew Farrell (1996-2004)
- 19 - Ellery Hanley (1985-1991)
- 17 - Alan Prescott (1955-1958)
- 15 - Jim Sullivan (1927-1933)
- 15 - Eric Ashton (1958-1963)
- 13 - Garry Schofield (1991-94)
- 11 - Jonty Parkin (1921-1930)
- 11 - Jamie Peacock (2005-2007)
- 10 - Harold Wagstaff (1914-1922)
- 11 - Roger Millward (1971-1978)
- 9 - Gus Risman (1936-1946)
- 9 - Ernest Ward (1947-1950)
- 9 - Frank Myler (1970)
- 9 - Clive Sullivan (1972-1973)
- 8 - Brian Noble (1984)
- 8 - Mike Gregory (1989-1990)
- 7 - James Lomas (1909-1912)
- 6 - Tommy Smales (1963-1965)
- 6 - Chris Hesketh (1974)
- 5 - Dickie Williams (1951-1954)
- 5 - Doug Laughton (1970-1979)
- 5 - George Nicholls (1979)
- 4 - Dave Valentine (1954)
- 4 - Jeff Stevenson (1959-1960)
- 4 - Eric Fraser (1960-1961)
- 4 - Harry Pinner (1985-1986)
- 4 - David Watkinson (1986)
- 4 - Shaun Edwards (1990-1994)
- 3 - Harry Taylor (1908)
- 3 - Willie Horne (1952)
- 3 - Ernie Ashcroft (1954)

- 3 - Alex Murphy (1964-1966)
- 3 - Neil Fox (1966-1968)
- 3 - Brian Edgar (1966)
- 3 - Bill Holliday (1967)
- 3 - Bev Risman (1968)

MIKE GREGORY and GARRY SCHOFIELD both led from the front as determined and distinguished captains of Great Britain.

- 3 - Len Casey (1980-1983)
- 2 - Gwyn Thomas (1920),
- 2 - Frank Gallagher (1924)
- 2 - Phil Jackson (1958)
- 2 - Johnny Whiteley (1959-1960)
- 2 - Derek Turner (1962)
- 2 - Harry Poole (1966)
- 2 - Alan Hardisty (1967)
- 2 - Tommy Bishop (1968-1969)
- 2 - George Fairbairn (1980)
- 2 - Jeff Grayshon (1980-1982)
- 1 - Bert Jenkins (1908)
- 1 - Johnny Thomas (1911)
- 1 - Les Fairclough (1929)
- 1 - Arthur Atkinson (1936)
- 1 - Jim Brough (1936)
- 1 - Tommy McCue (1946)
- 1 - Ted Ward (1947)
- 1 - Joe Egan (1947)
- 1 - Jack Cunliffe (1951)
- 1 - Syd Hynes (1971)
- 1 - David Ward (1981)
- 1 - Steve Nash (1982)
- 1 - David Topliss (1982)
- 1 - Keith Mumby (1984)
- 1 - Andy Goodway (1885),
- 1 - Jonathan Davies (1992)
- 1 - Andy Platt (1993),
- 1 - Philip Clarke (1994)
- 1 - Paul Sculthorpe (2006)
- 1 - Adrian Morley (2007).

A CENTURY of GREAT BRITAIN

Bringing down the curtain on a Rugby League institution

The Great Britain team - the name that for generations had become synonymous with Rugby League's best at international level - was put "on ice" at the end of 2007. Official policy now appears to be that "England" will contest all future home Test series, but the Great Britain team could still be resurrected to undertake a Lions tour down-under. As there have been no genuine Lions tours to Australia since the introduction of Super League's summer rugby (the last one was in 1992) nobody will be holding their breath wondering when the next tour might be.

Nobody can take away the game's memories of the past and the records achieved by British teams throughout the last century are written in stone. Through the guises of "The Northern Union," "England" and "Great Britain," our British teams have represented our nation, and our game, in many dramatic events laced with rare feats of courage and great skill. Those records of the most Great Britain appearances and top try and goal scorers are printed on this page. Test matches have been played against Australia, New Zealand, France, Papua New Guinea and Fiji - and, for the purpose of the records in this book, the series against the so-called Australian Super League team in 1997 are included.

As the last Great Britain Test series approached in 2007, the Rugby Football League organised a website poll to select a "greatest ever" Great Britain player, with Ellery Hanley coming out at number one. Ellery is pictured (left) receiving a memento to mark that achievement in 2007. No doubt most of those who cast votes would be from a younger generation to whom the many great names of the past would mean little - that is only natural. But from James Lomas and Harold Wagstaff to Ellery Hanley, the honour of leading the British team has always meant everything.

MOST CAPPED G.B. PLAYERS

25 or more appearances

46 -	Mick Sullivan	(1954-1963)
46 (2)	Garry Schofield	(1984-1994)
36 (1)	Ellery Hanley	(1984-1993)
36 (4)	Shaun Edwards	(1985-1994)
34	Andrew Farrell	(1993-2004)
33	Martin Offiah	(1988-1994)
33(2)	Keith Senior	(1996-2007)
33(10)	Daryl Powell	(1990-1996)
32(2)	Denis Betts	(1990-1999)
31	Billy Boston	(1954-1963)
31(3)	Garry Connolly	(1991-2003)
30(1)	Cliff Watson	(1963-1971)
30(7)	Joe Lydon	(1983-1992)
30(6)	Adrian Morley	(1996-2007)
29	George Nicholls	(1971-1979)
29	Neil Fox	(1959-1969)
29(1)	Roger Millward	(1966-1978)
28	Alan Prescott	(1951-1958)
27	Phil Jackson	(1954-1958)
27	Alex Murphy	(1958-1971)
26	Eric Ashton	(1957-1963)
26	John Atkinson	(1968-1980)
26(1)	Andy Gregory	(1981-1992)
26(3)	Jamie Peacock	(2001-2007)
25	Brian McTigue	(1958-1963)
25	Jim Sullivan	(1924-1933)
25	Tommy Harris	(1954-1960)
25(3)	Stuart Fielden	(2001-2006)
25(4)	Andy Platt	(1985-1993)

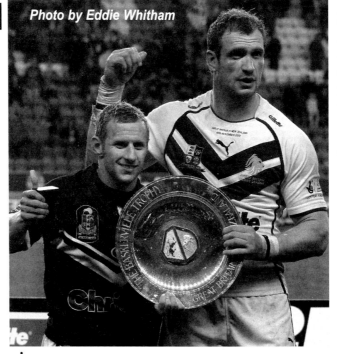

Photo by Eddie Whitham

(Left) The final moment for Great Britain at the end of the 2007 Test series with the Kiwis. Captain Jamie Peacock holds the Baskerville Shield, whilst Rob Burrow has the George Smith medal as player-of-the-series. Both trophies in memory of the "All Golds" pioneers of a century before.

Top 10 try-scorers

41	Mick Sullivan
31	Garry Schofield
26	Martin Offiah
24	Billy Boston
20	Ellery Hanley
17	Roger Millward
16	Alex Murphy
15	Shaun Edwards
14	Eric Ashton
14	Neil Fox

Top 10 goal-kickers

93	Neil Fox
66	Lewis Jones
64	Jim Sullivan
59	Andrew Farrell
53	Eric Fraser
49	Jonathan Davies
44	George Fairbairn
39	Paul Eastwood
31	Paul Loughlin
27	Bobbie Goulding

Memories of the WIRE

Photos by EDDIE WHITHAM

(Above) Warrington hero MIKE GREGORY making a brave attempt to stop "Guru" Eric Grothe during his spell with Leeds in 1984. *(Left)* KEN KELLY and STEVE HESFORD winning the John Player Trophy in 1981. *(Below)* Warrington team in 1986. Left to right, *back row):* Tony Barrow (coach), Joe Ropati, Tony Thorniley, Mark Roberts, Ronnie Duane, Bob Eccles, Kevin Tamati, Mike Gregory, Brian Johnson. *(Front row):* Bob Jackson, Paul Cullen, Les Boyd, Paul Bishop, ANO, Andy Gregory, Ken Kelly.

LEEDS LOYALTY

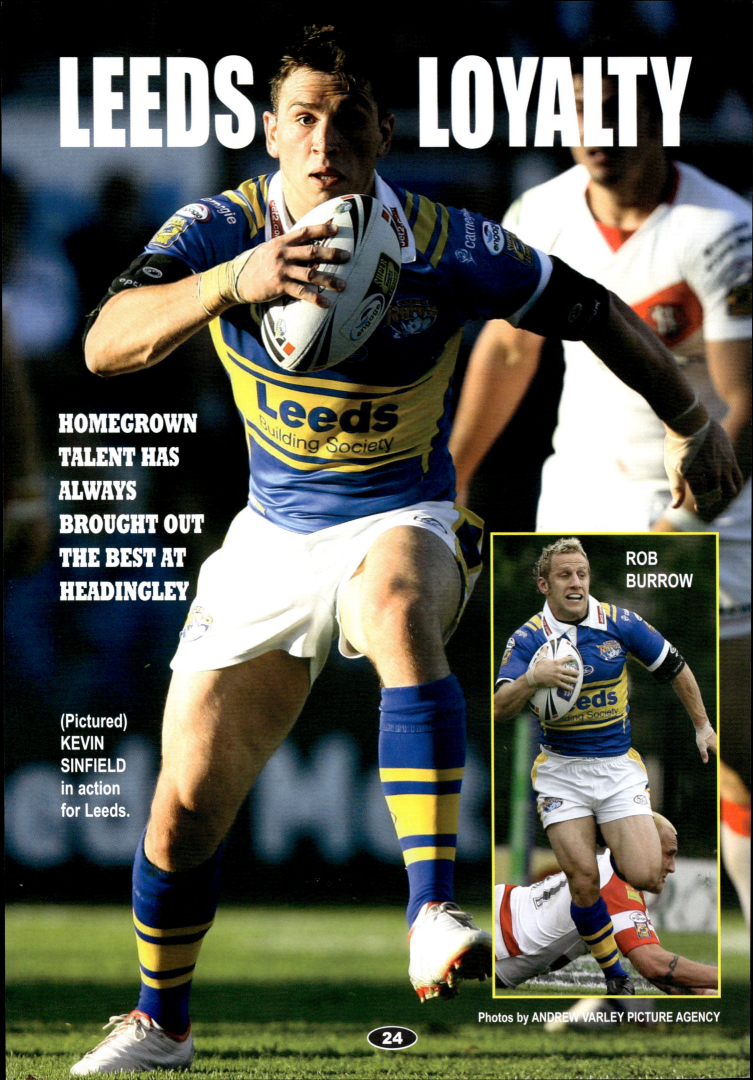

HOMEGROWN TALENT HAS ALWAYS BROUGHT OUT THE BEST AT HEADINGLEY

(Pictured) KEVIN SINFIELD in action for Leeds.

ROB BURROW

Photos by ANDREW VARLEY PICTURE AGENCY

(Above) **JOHN HOLMES**, the ultimate "local lad makes good at Headingley" story, pictured diving over for one of his 150-plus tries for the Loiners.

As Leeds clinched Grand Final victory at Old Trafford in 2008 they wrote themselves into the Headingley record books as the first Leeds team to win back-to-back Championships in the long and illustrious history of the club. And a look at the Leeds side in 2008 reveals, just as they did when they won their first Championships under Joe Warham in 1961 and 1969, that title-winning Leeds teams are always built on homegrown talent.

Whilst some Super League clubs are awash with imported Antipodeans, Leeds have been much more judicious in their signings from overseas, with much more emphasis being put on the development of their own young players recuited from Yorkshire junior football. No individual typifies that homegrown feeling more than Danny McGuire, a city boy who learned his rugby with the East Leeds amateur club, before stepping into the shoes of his heroes at Headingley. In making the coveted number six jersey his own, Danny is carrying on a tradition laid down by other great Leeds stand-offs like John Holmes, Mick Shoebottom and Garry Schofield. The latter two came from south of the river in Hunslet country, but the boy prodigy Holmes (who made his first team debut aged just 16) was schooled on the doorstep of Headingley at Burley Road and Kirkstall.

Obviously the Leeds local scouting system is working as well as ever, just as it did when Joe Warham and company were masterminding their Headingley talent development programmes in the 1960s. Joe had a network of contacts who would "tip him off" about promising young

(Above) **DANNY McGUIRE**, former East Leeds boy who has made the number six jersey his own at Headingley.

players, and among the Leeds scouts was Tommy Bailey, the man who discovered future captain Syd Hynes, among plenty of others. It was one of Joe Warham's personal contacts, a former team-mate in playing days at Swinton named Billy Riley, who masterminded the influx of talented signings by Leeds from the city of York. Billy had played for York and settled in the Minster City, and acted as Leeds scout among the local juniors to keep Joe informed of promising players. The result was such good players as: Vince Hattee, Danny Sheehan, Geoff Wrigglesworth, Ray Batten (the latter two both became Test players) and Ted Barnard all travelling from York to Leeds. Such was the pulling power of Headingley, which remains to this day.

THE GOLDEN BOYS

One of publisher Harry Edgar's proudest achievements during the lifetime of the former *"Open Rugby"* magazine was the creation of the Golden Boot award - presented to the world's number one player.

The award became recognised as the most prestigious individual accolade in world Rugby League, supported by global sporting giants *Adidas* and a creator of many press headlines in Australia, New Zealand and France as well as in Great Britain. The first Golden Boot award winner was Wally Lewis, who received the glittering prize in his home city of Brisbane in 1985. Subsequent winners were: Brett Kenny (Australia) in 1986; Gary Jack (Australia) in 1987; Hugh McGahan (New Zealand) in 1988, shared with Peter Sterling (Australia); Ellery Hanley (Great Britain) in 1989; and Mal Meninga (Australia) in 1990. The award was suspended in 1991 when *"Open Rugby"* firmly believed the Golden Boot should have been won by Great Britain's Garry Schofield, but the Australian partners in the event would not agree to a British winner.

So, 1985 to 1990 were the golden years. But we have always wondered what an incredible roll of honour could have been created if we had been able to present the Golden Boot in the years before 1985. Now, in what might be the most audacious of examples of fantasy football, we are presenting the men who would have been our choice as the Golden Boot winners as the world's most outstanding players in every post-War year from 1946 leading up to the award's actual creation in 1985.

The Golden Boot
Roll of honour as the World's best in Post-War years

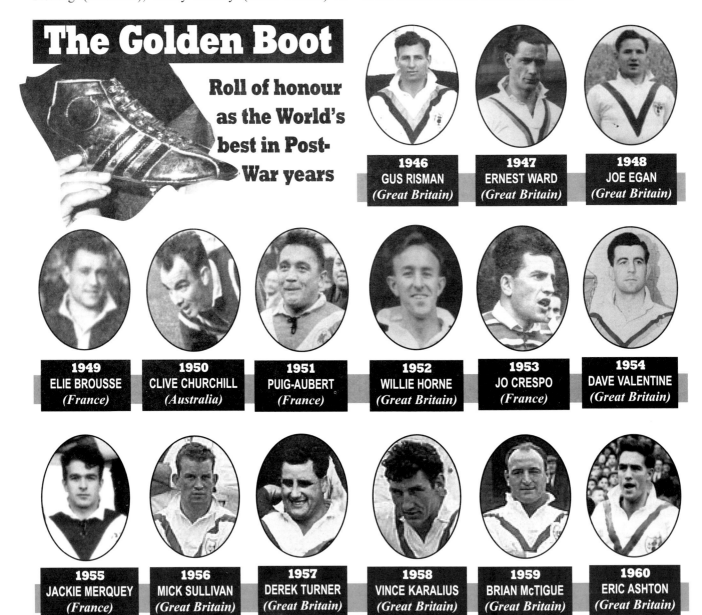

1946 GUS RISMAN *(Great Britain)*
1947 ERNEST WARD *(Great Britain)*
1948 JOE EGAN *(Great Britain)*
1949 ELIE BROUSSE *(France)*
1950 CLIVE CHURCHILL *(Australia)*
1951 PUIG-AUBERT *(France)*
1952 WILLIE HORNE *(Great Britain)*
1953 JO CRESPO *(France)*
1954 DAVE VALENTINE *(Great Britain)*
1955 JACKIE MERQUEY *(France)*
1956 MICK SULLIVAN *(Great Britain)*
1957 DEREK TURNER *(Great Britain)*
1958 VINCE KARALIUS *(Great Britain)*
1959 BRIAN McTIGUE *(Great Britain)*
1960 ERIC ASHTON *(Great Britain)*

OF WORLD RUGBY

An exercise in fantasy football - or a reflection of where the strength lay in world Rugby League in years gone by? In the 39 players nominated from the years 1946 to 1984, there are 19 from Great Britain, 13 from Australia, 4 from France and 3 from New Zealand.

1961 DICK HUDDART *(Great Britain)*

1962 ALEX MURPHY *(Great Britain)*

1963 REG GASNIER *(Australia)*

1964 IAN WALSH *(Australia)*

1965 TOMMY SMALES *(Great Britain)*

1966 TOMMY BISHOP *(Great Britain)*

1967 GRM. LANGLANDS *(Australia)*

1968 JOHNNY RAPER *(Australia)*

1969 MAL REILLY *(Great Britain)*

1970 ROGER MILLWARD *(Great Britain)*

1971 PHIL ORCHARD *(New Zealand)*

1972 MIKE STEPHENSON *(Great Britain)*

1973 BOB FULTON *(Australia)*

1974 RON COOTE *(Australia)*

1975 ARTHUR BEETSON *(Australia)*

1976 GEORGE NICHOLLS *(Great Britain)*

1977 STEVE NASH *(Great Britain)*

1978 GRAHAM EADIE *(Australia)*

1979 ROD REDDY *(Australia)*

1980 FRED AH KUOI *(New Zealand)*

1981 STEVE ROGERS *(Australia)*

1982 PETER STERLING *(Australia)*

1983 MARK GRAHAM *(New Zealand)*

1984 WAYNE PEARCE *(Australia)*

THE REMARKABLE STORY OF JOE LEVULA AND THE FIJIAN STARS OF THE SIXTIES

Joe's leap from FIJI TO ROCHDALE

Rochdale Hornets were the instigators of one of the most remarkable stories in British sport in the early 1960s when they opened the doors for Fijian rugby players to come to the so-called "mother country."

When the Hornets announced in the autumn of 1961 that they were recruiting a couple of Rugby Union players from the Pacific island land of Fiji, they began exploring an avenue that would bring to Rugby League in the north of England a whole new colony of wonderfully exotic names which quickly became familiar to the game's followers, despite their difficulty in pronouncing them.

The adventure started when the Rochdale Hornets club placed a very speculative advertisement in the *"Fiji Times"* newspaper, seeking rugby players interested in the opportunity to play as professionals in England. Much of Rugby League's appeal throughout its history had been based on the English clubs' ability to recruit players from overseas, with many of them becoming star attractions - the charisma of being from a faraway place with a faraway accent adding hugely to their footballing prowess.

So when the primary sources of overseas stars were cut off by a ban on signing Rugby League players from both Australia and New Zealand, the English clubs had turned their recruiting eyes to nations where Rugby Union was the only game open to players. Thus, South Africa became a major recruiting ground in the late 1950s and then, in its constant pursuit of the next new thing, Rugby League discovered Fiji.

The first two Fijian players arrived in Rochdale on 13th October, 1961 with the Hornets officials who met them blissfully unaware of the true status in their homeland of the two men they had recruited - Orisi Dawai and Josefa (Joe) Levula. Dawai was the former captain of the Fiji national Rugby Union team, and had led them on successful tours to both Australia and New Zealand in the 1950s, whilst the giant winger Levula was regarded as the greatest sportsman Fiji had ever known.

In later years it emerged that Joe Levula was known as *"the Pele of Fiji"* and his potential as a Rugby League crowd-puller had first been uncovered over a decade earlier by none other than the famous broadcaster and journalist Eddie Waring. It was whilst in Australia, where he was reporting on the 1950 Lions tour, that Eddie claimed to have first seen the young Levula play. A year later, Joe had made his Rugby Union Test debut for Fiji in New Zealand and by the end of 1951 was voted by the *"New Zealand Rugby Alamanack"* as the best winger in the world. Eddie tipped off numerous English Rugby League clubs about this exciting Fijian prospect, but nothing came of it and Joe continued to cement his reputation at home.

WELCOME TO ROCHDALE - the Hornets coach in 1961, Fred Selway, gives a quick introduction to Lancashire and Rugby League to Joe Levula (left) and Orisi Dawai shortly after their arrival from Fiji. Note the traditional dress of the Fijians. *(Left)* Dawai and Levula in action in their debuts for Rochdale.

The appearance of Dawai and Levula in the Rochdale team immediately became a talking point throughout the Rugby League - not least because their first sighting in the Lancashire cotton town saw them wearing traditional Fijian dress of skirts below their blazers. Levula soon made an impact, his long, loping stride playing havoc with opposing defences and making him a big attraction wherever the Hornets played.

Rochdale wasted little time in recruiting another two Fijians - both mighty forwards this time - and Laitia Ravouvou and Voate Drui arrived in February, 1962. By Christmas of that year, the Hornets chairman Arthur Walker had increased the club's Fijian colony to six with the signing of threequarters Litai Burogolevu and Gideon Dolo - neither of whom ever played in the first team.

The Hornets were to sign another forward a couple of years later in early 1964 who proved to be the most effective of all the Fijian players - his name was Apisia Toga and in his four seasons at the Athletic Grounds he became one of the most powerful running forwards in the British game. Toga knew his worth and, eventually, negotiated a transfer to Australia where he played over 100 games for the top Sydney club, the mighty St.George, before meeting a tragic early death after collapsing from a heart attack during pre-season training in 1973.

Mike Ratu became the next successful Fijian recruit at Rochdale when he joined Hornets in 1965 and enjoyed a good career as a winger following in the huge footsteps of his boyhood hero, Joe Levula. In the four decades that have passed since the first Fijians were sighted in Rochdale, nobody has done more than Mike to maintain the ties that bind by organising regular re-unions. And while Rochdale will always be the town most associated with the Fijians, some guests at those re-unions over the years have travelled from other towns in Lancashire and Yorkshire which became their homes after other Rugby League clubs followed the lead set by the Hornets.

Huddersfield were one such club when they signed four Fijians in 1964: Joe Saukuru, Tom Waqabaca, John Ravitale and Tom Naidole. And Wigan put the seal of approval on Fijian signings when, in 1963, they recruited a stand-off called Kaiava Qasote Bosenavulagi - better known simply as Kia Bose. He accepted Wigan's invitation to join them in late 1962, leaving his job in the Government printing office in Suva to travel to Lancashire where he arrived right in the middle in one of the worst winters ever known in the north of England. There were memorable newspaper photographs of Kia taking his first look at Central Park skating on the fozen surface, whilst in the background workmen with pneumatic drills were trying to break the ice.

Kia Bose played only one first team game for Wigan before moving to Blackpool Borough where he enjoyed an excellent career spread over six seasons, confirming his reputation as a player with fine handling skills and a drop-goal expert. During his time with Blackpool, Bose was joined by a fellow Fijian, Johnny Nabou - a loose-forward and former national wrestling champion who had been brought to England by the Borough chairman Gordon Emery after he had read a magazine article about the 1961 Fijian Rugby Union touring team to Australia in which Nabou was rated the outstanding player.

Tragically, Orisi Dawai died suddenly in 1966, just five years after arriving in Rochdale, at the reported age of only thirty-three. The great Joe Levula and Laitia Ravouvou were also to meet their eventual fate in Rochdale without ever stepping foot again on their native Fijian soil. Happily, Kia Bose has continued to enjoy a long and happy life in his adopted town of Wigan, and been able to re-visit Fiji on family holidays.

ONE OF RUGBY LEAGUE'S GREATEST FAMILY DYNASTIES

The Battens

Three generations of British international players

(Above) The man who started it all - the legendary Billy Batten, pictured at Hull with the Challenge Cup in 1914.

The spectacular action shot *(above)* remains one of the most famous Rugby League pictures ever taken. It was snapped by a Yorkshire newspaper photographer, Lorne Green, on the midweek evening in 1947 when a record crowd of 40,175 gathered at Headingley to see Leeds play Bradford Northern in a league fixture.

The picture captures the famous "Batten leap" more vividly than any other as Bradford's international winger Eric Batten shows his hurdling technique in an image that will be familiar to most people who have studied the game's history. What is less well known is that the Leeds defender left grasping thin air as the Bradford man flies over him, is none other than Eric Batten's own brother Bob. You see, Rugby League always was a family affair for the Battens.

Three generations of Battens with British international honours set a remarkable record. It all began with the great Billy Batten in the years before the First World War when this most powerful of threequarters became a giant of the then Northern Union.

Hailing from the Yorkshire mining village of Fitzwilliam, Billy starred for Hunslet, Hull and later Wakefield Trinity in a footballing career that made him one of the true legends of the game, and an automatic entrant to the original "Hall of Fame." His three sons - Eric, Bob and Billy - were all prominent Rugby League players, with Eric following in the footsteps of his father as an international. Billy Batten senior has been one of the original Lions tourists in 1910, and son Eric was a member of the *"Indomitables"* in 1946 after the War had prevented him making what would almost certainly have been his first tour in 1940.

Like father Billy, Eric Batten first made his name playing for Hunslet then, after the War, he starred for Bradford Northern and became one of the great personalities during the game's "golden era" of big crowds and great players. He joined Featherstone Rovers as their player-coach in 1951 at the age of 36, and proceeded to guide them - from his position on the wing - to Wembley in 1952. It was a first for Featherstone but this was Eric Batten's fourth Wembley Cup Final and, despite being in his late 'thirties he went on to score no less than 60 tries in 101 games for the Rovers.

Eric was Billy Batten's second son, and like his father he developed the skill of being able to leap clean over opponents who went in for a low tackle. The Batten "leap" became a trademark that thrilled the crowds who waited for it to happen with great anticipation. In later years, Eric Batten would always recall the stories of his father from the first Lions tour in 1910 - a tour in which he came up against the famous Maori Opai Asher, another powerful man also reknowned for his hurdling over opponents.

"All they heard when they got to Australia was 'wait until you meet Opai Asher,'" remembered Eric. "He was the man they all feared, but not my dad. The first match they played against each other, Billy went up to leap and Opai Asher went up to leap and stop him - they met in mid-air and they had to carry him (Asher) off, he was concussed and needed stitches in his head."

The youngest of Billy Batten's three sons, Bob, died earlier in 2008 at the age of 81. He had enjoyed a solid Rugby League career of his own without reaching the dizzy heights of his father or brother Eric. Bob Batten played first as a stand-off before continuing the Batten family tradition as a three-quarter for Leeds, Oldham and Castleford. His eldest brother, Billy Batten 2nd, provided a third generation of international Battens when his son, Ray, went on to be one of the finest footballers ever to grace the Leeds colours.

Loose-forward Ray Batten signed for Leeds as a 17-year-old from the York amateur club Heworth, in 1963. By the time he wound down his magnficient career at Headingley 13 years later in 1976, he had played 420 first team games in the blue and amber making him one of Leeds's greatest servants. With three Test matches for Great Britain and four England appearances, he followed in the footsteps of his famous grandfather and Uncle Eric, although Ray did not inherit their showmanship and was

(Above) **RAY BATTEN the very talented Leeds loose-forward.**

Billy Batten's other two sons. *(Left)* BOB BATTEN and *(far left)* BILLY BATTEN 2nd. - the father of international Ray Batten.

always regarded as a quiet character who let his skills do all his talking on the field as he carved open opposing defences for the benefit of his supporting team-mates. None moresoe than second-rower Bob Haigh when he set a new try-scoring record for a forward with 40 touchdowns in the 1970-71 season - the vast majority of them coming direct from openings set up by the passes of his back-row partner Ray Batten.

The man who signed Ray as a professional, the then Leeds manager Joe Warham, once revealed some Batten family influences at work. "There was some dispute as to Ray's best position," recalled Joe. "His father maintained that half-back was his role and many others, good judges, took this view in his early career. For my part, there was never any doubt. It was as a ball-playing forward. I signed him, and if ever Ray were to move from number 13, I'm sure it would be up front where he might eventually emulate the feats of great ball workers like Egan and Slevin.

"There was a unique clause written into Ray Batten's agreement. It appeared that only twice in history had a player captained Yorkshire to a hat-trick of victories in the County Championship. On each occasion it had been a Batten, and the feat was recognised by the presentation of a jewelled centre to the County medal. Ray's father, Billy, was adamant that should Ray repeat the achievement some similar recognition be given."

Jewels in the crown may be a well worn cliche, but nobody can deny that in the history of Rugby League, the Battens truly were among the crown jewels.

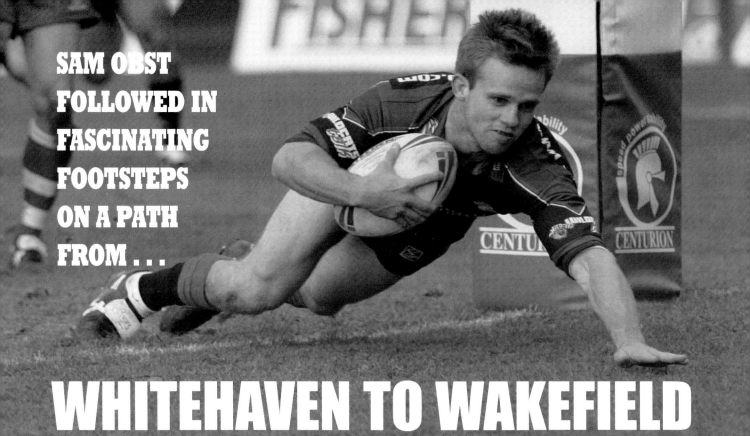

SAM OBST FOLLOWED IN FASCINATING FOOTSTEPS ON A PATH FROM...

WHITEHAVEN TO WAKEFIELD

Present day followers of Wakefield Trinity may not have been aware of it when their club signed Sam Obst from Whitehaven, but the little Aussie was following in some fascinating footsteps on what might seem like an unlikely path from West Cumbria to Belle Vue and the Merrie City.

Obst, whose father Tony was a very well known Brisbane player and became a big favourite at Keighley when he guested at Lawkholme Lane in the 1970s, was introduced to English Rugby League by Whitehaven in 2004. Sam wasted little time in showing his talents in a 'Haven team that went to within just a couple of minutes of winning a place in Super League when a Leigh drop-goal forced a draw against them in the National League One Grand Final. Obst was voted the National League player-of-the-year for the 2004 season and immediately became a target for some of the bigger clubs.

He is still fondly remembered by Whitehaven fans and former team-mates who find it rather sad that the scrum-half they knew with such marvellously creative passing and kicking skills - straight out of the Peter Sterling mould - appears to have spent most of his ensuing career with Wakefield restricted to playing as an interchange hooker.

Sam Obst was joined at Wakefield in 2008 by another former Whitehaven player in forward Oliver Wilkes, but can Trinity fans remember some of the others who arrived at Belle Vue from the Cumbrian club in years gone by?

One of the first was the big second-rower Dennis Williamson, who was transferred to Wakefield in 1961 and by the end of his first season in Yorkshire was a Wembley winner as Trinity beat Huddersfield in the 1962 Challenge Cup Final. Williamson partnered Brian Briggs in the engine-room of the pack as Wakefield won 12-6 in a Final

ALAN McCURRIE in action for Wakefield in the 1981-82 season. The skilful hooker was recruited by Trinity after he made his name with hometown club Whitehaven.

in which Neil Fox kicked three drop-goals and won the Lance Todd Trophy. Within a year, Dennis Williamson had returned to Whitehaven, his Wembley winners' medal

WAKEFIELD TRINITY IN 1968 - SPOT THE THREE EX-WHITEHAVEN PLAYERS

The Wakefield Trinity team in 1968-69 season *(above)* are, left to right: *(Standing):* Matt McLeod, Ted Campbell, David Jeanes, Terry Ramshaw, David Hawley, Bob Haigh, Tom Hill, Don Fox. *(Seated):* Gary Cooper, Geoff Wraith, Ian Brooke, Neil Fox (captain), Richard Paley, Keith Slater, Ken Hirst. *(In front):* Ken Batty and Joe Bonnar.

DENNIS WILLIAMSON *(right)* playing for Wakefield in the 1962 Cup Final at Wembley, looks on as Trinity pack-mate Brian Briggs is tackled by Huddersfield's Mick Clarke.

safely in his pocket. Not quite so lucky was Matt McLeod, another second-rower who left Whitehaven for Wakefield and also played at Wembley in his first season. But that was the 1968 "Watersplash" Final and McLeod, who must have been a strong contender for the Lance Todd trophy with his powerful display that day, will always be remembered as the man who put a consoling arm around the shoulders of the distraught Don Fox as they walked off the pitch on that fateful afternoon.

Matt had moved to Wakefield at the end of 1967 around the same time as scrum-half Joe Bonnar - a very talented 19-year-old who had come to Trinity's attention in a County match for Cumberland against Yorkshire. Joe went on to give many years fine service to Wakefield, and the following season in 1968-69, McLeod and Bonnar were joined by another of their old Whitehaven teammates, the very experienced County hooker Tom Hill whose job in the civil service was taking him to West Yorkshire. Not quite so well known is that around the same time in 1968, a couple of other Whitehaven forwards appeared in Wakefield's first team on a trial basis - Niah Vaughan and Tom Fowler. Vaughan, who played more games for Trinity, had been at prop in the Whitehaven team which beat the New Zealanders in 1965 and, in later years, gained fame as a solo round-the-world yachtsman. He also gained some notoriety as a restaurant owner in in his home town and was last heard of running an orange grove in South Africa.

It was always reckoned that Jim Brough, the former G.B. captain and coach, was Trinity's scout when it came to recruiting all these players from Cumberland. But Jim's scouting days had passed by the time hooker Alan McCurrie left Whitehaven for Wakefield and he, too, was soon at Wembley in the Trinity team led by David Topliss which lost to Widnes in the 1979 Cup Final.

Building the reputation

St.Helens have enjoyed great success in recent years, but here's a reminder of some of those who helped build the Saints fine reputation in years gone by.

(Above) Ray French on the charge for Saints in the 1965 Championship Final against Halifax at Swinton's Station Road. Ray is trying to avoid a tackle by loose-forward Charlie Renilson as St.Helens half-back Wilf Smith and Halifax forward Ken Roberts look ready to offer a helping hand. That wasn't a glory day for Saints as Halifax won 15-7 to clinch the title after coming from seventh place to overcome league leaders St.Helens in the play-offs.

(Right) A happier day for the Saints as they won the Challenge Cup at Wembley in 1976 when all the pre-match tipsters reckoned Widnes would be too fit and too fast for an older St.Helens pack. With Welsh veterans Kel Coslett and John Mantle playing like men possessed as props in the sweltering heat of a Wembley scorcher, Saints beat Widnes 20-5 in front of an 89,982 crowd. Just to stir a few more memories, the St.Helens team that day was: **Geoff Pimblett; Les Jones, Eddie Cunningham, Derek Noonan, Roy Mathias; Billy Benyon, Jeff Heaton; John Mantle, Tony Karalius, Kel Coslett, George Nicholls, Eric Chisnall, David Hull. Subs: Peter Glynn and Mel James.**

SAINTS *style*

SEAN LONG *(above)* has been a key factor in the Saints' run of success in the Super League era - yet, irony or ironies, he is a Wiganer, infamously let go to Widnes before he found his way to Knowsley Road and St.Helens stardom.

Photos by ANDREW VARLEY PICTURE AGENCY

JON WILKIN *(above)* is very much the prototype of the modern day professional Rugby League player in the 21st Century, where specialist roles are a thing of the past and multi-skilled athletes alternate between backs and forwards. The former Hull K.R. player, Wilkin is one of the game's best all-rounders.

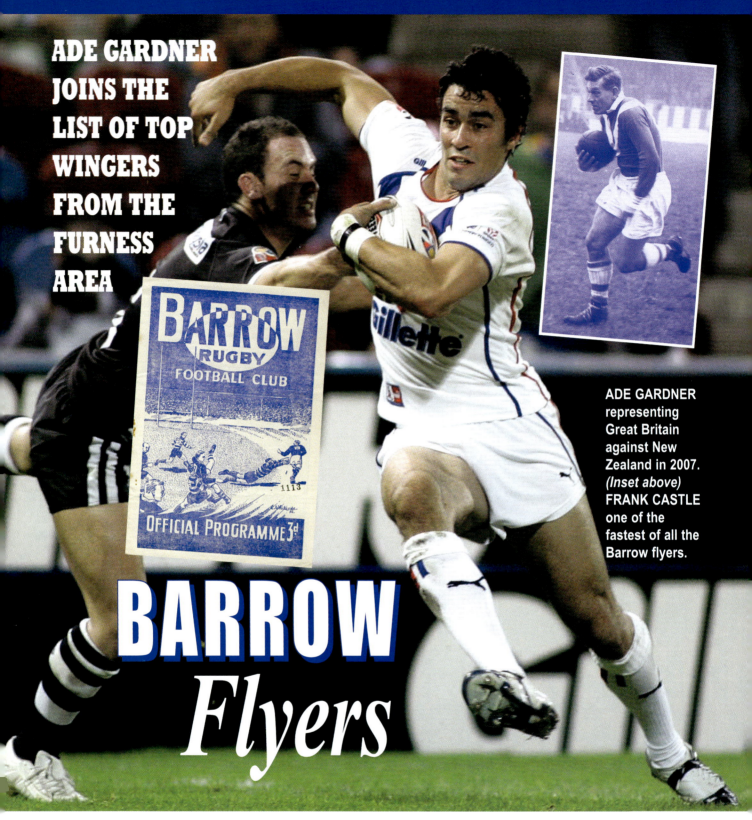

ADE GARDNER JOINS THE LIST OF TOP WINGERS FROM THE FURNESS AREA

ADE GARDNER representing Great Britain against New Zealand in 2007. *(Inset above)* FRANK CASTLE one of the fastest of all the Barrow flyers.

BARROW *Flyers*

The former Barrow winger Ade Gardner has proved to be a real success story since he joined St.Helens. At a time when top British born wings are few and far between in the Super League, Gardner has played a significant role in the many Saints' trophy wins, established himself as a first choice Great Britain (and now England) international, and become the top try-scorer in the Super League. In doing so, Gardner has continued to uphold the tradition of the Barrow club for producing top-class wing-threequarters.

The list of flyers who thrilled the crowds at Craven Park with their exploits down the flanks will bring a warm glow of satisfaction to those Barrow fans old enough to remember. Legend will have told them about pre-War favourites like "Tot" Wallace, Val Cumberbatch, "Tank" Woods and the sprinter "Grav" Johnston - but even they would pale in comparison to the stars who were to follow. None were better than the trio of Jimmy Lewthwaite, Frank Castle and Bill Burgess, who all wore international colours but will always be synonymous with the famous Barrow blue

(Main picture, above) BILL BURGESS dives over to score in familiar style for England against France in a 1969 international at Central Park. *(Insets)* JIMMY LEWTHWAITE in international kit and LES QUIRK playing for St.Helens.

jersey with the white vee. In more recent times in the 1980s, Les Quirk paved the way for Ade Gardner to move from Barrow to St.Helens and he, too, became a big favourite with the Knowsley Road crowds. The Amateur clubs of the Furness area have always been among the best in the country and they can be proud of these two products - Quirk came from Dalton and Gardner from Barrow Island. Another more recent Barrow winger, Paul Salmon, also appeared to have all the potential to reach the top before injury halted his career.

But any discussion on Barrow wingers will always come back to Lewthwaite, Castle and Burgess. They were great wingers in anybody's language. All three played at Wembley for Barrow and were internationals in the days when Great Britain knew they could win the Ashes. Lewthwaite and Castle even played together as England's wingers and were part of an all international threequarter line at Craven Park when Phil Jackson and Dennis Goodwin were their centres.

Lewthwaite and Castle both gave incredible service to the Barrow club. Jimmy was a Cumbrian who hailed from Cleator Moor and had moved to Barrow in search of work before the War. He was better known as a soccer player before he went to Craven Park, but he went on to play a record 501 first team games for Barrow in a 15-season career in which he scored a club record 353 tries. At international level Jimmy never got to play in a Test match for Great Britain, yet he was the leading try-scorer on the famous 1946 *"Indomitables"* tour. He brought the curtain down on his marvellous career in the 1957 Cup Final at Wembley, at the end of a campaign in which - at the age of 35 - he had set a new Barrow tries-in-a-season record.

His wing partner Frank Castle didn't have Jimmy's physical presence, but he was one of the fastest players the game has ever seen. Frank signed for Barrow from the Coventry Rugby Union club in 1949 and wasted no time in confirming that he was something special, thrilling the crowds with his lightening pace. In 11 seasons with Barrow, Frank scored 281 tries in 366 games - he also played for the Ashes-winning Great Britain team in 1952 and was a Lions tourist in 1954.

But, perhaps, even Lewthwaite and Castle would have to bow the knee to Bill Burgess when selecting Barrow's best ever winger. Certainly Bill's try-scoring average is slightly ahead of his famous predecessors, with 179 tries in 222 games providing an average of one try every 1.24 games, despite Barrow no longer being a top side by the time he joined them. His career at Craven Park was shorter because, at the height of his fame, Burgess was signed by the then big-spending Salford club. Bill won 14 Great Britain caps between 1962 and 1969, all before joining Salford, and he also represented England on several occasions. He emulated his famous father by also becoming a Lions tourist in 1966, and for some time was regarded by many wise judges and fellow players as the best winger in the world. Certainly few other wingers of his era could match his ability to beat defenders in a tight space with brilliant acceleration and change of pace.

For much of his time at Barrow, Bill Burgess formed a devastating wing partnership with another real speed-merchant, Mike Murray, the one time Powderhall sprint champion. Murray had the potential to be an Olympic finalist as a sprinter and certainly gave real substance to the description: "Barrow flyers."

Remembering Rugby League's spirit of adventure

GOING OUT ON THE ROAD

THERE was a time when English Rugby League teams were in demand outside the game's local strongholds and the Rugby Football League, under the guidance of its Secretary Bill Fallowfield, was a governing body always happy to accept an opportunity to promote the game to a new audience.

Numerous propaganda matches were staged in Wales, not least a week long tour in May, 1949 by the Huddersfield and St.Helens clubs, in which they played three exhibition matches in different towns (including one at the Brewery Field, Bridgend - home of the present day Celtic Crusaders), and on the nights in between staged *"Focus on Rugby"* meetings with guest speakers in Cardiff and in Ystradgynlais. This venture was arranged by the Welsh Rugby League Commission.

Elsewhere - whilst in recent years there has been a growing interest in Rugby League as a participation sport at amateur level in both Ireland and South Africa - back in the 1950s and early 'sixties, promoters in both these countries were keen to attract professional teams from England to play exhibition matches for which they knew they could attract good crowds. In the case of South Africa it was part of a belief that the Rugby League game could take off and become established as a high level sport in that country; whereas in Ireland there were no such plans and it was just a matter of Rugby League being seen as a good money-maker for local Irish causes.

Halifax and Warrington were the first to accept a post-War invitation to play in Ireland in 1954. The R.F.L. had been approached by the Marist Fathers of Milltown to stage a match in Dublin with a view to raising funds for a new church, and this took place at Dalymount Park, home of Bohemians Football Club on the evening of Friday 28th May, 1954. It should be remembered that Halifax and Warrington had recently played against each other in both the Championship and Challenge Cup Finals plus, of course, the famous replay at Odsal. So enthused was the R.F.L. secretary Bill Fallowfield that he used his own personal contacts (gained whilst in Ulster on R.A.F. duties during the War) to arrange an additional game between Halifax and Warrington in Northern Ireland. This was staged at Belfast's famous Windsor Park on the Thursday evening, 24 hours before the Dublin event.

A crowd of over 15,000 Dubliners turned out at Dalymount Park and newspaper reports stated they had left the ground *"elated with the feast of Rugby served up by Halifax and Warrington. They saw more open football and slick passing than they would normally expect in a whole season of Irish club Rugby (Union)."*

The match certainly was a successful venture for the organisers, the Marist Fathers. They had guaranteed the Halifax and Warrington clubs £300 each for expenses on top of their own match expenses, and the 15,000 crowd provided a "gate" of £1,378 to pay all this and leave a good profit for the church funds.

Meanwhile, first steps into South Africa were taken three years later, in 1957. Bill Fallowfield

Programmes from 1962 summer overseas ventures. *(Left)* Wakefield Trinity in South Africa and *(above right)* the Irish tournament in County Dublin involving four English clubs.

had responded positively to the overtures of a syndicate based in Johannesburg who wanted to promote Rugby League in South Africa, and had first met with their spokesman, a Mr. Ludwig Japhet, as early as December, 1953, in London. The eventual result was an arrangement for the Great Britain and France international teams to travel to South Africa *en-route* home from the 1957 World Cup in Australia, and play three matches against each other in Benoni, Durban and East London.

The games were well attended and, according to Mr.Fallowfield, extremely well publicised in the South African press. But, alas, the quality of play was very disappointing with the teams indulging in exhibition-type rugby and big scores being run up - which did not appeal to the South African public who liked their rugby a lot

(Above) Photographic evidence of Great Britain playing France in South Africa in 1957 has rarely been seen, but here's action from one of the three matches played on a sun-baked pitch in the Republic. The British player in the centre of the action is Geoff Gunney and, as you can see from the picture, they really did draw a crowd back then in South Africa.

more hard and rugged. Sadly, Ludwig Japhet died only a few weeks after the 1957 visit by the British and French teams and, without him, this initial attempt to promote the game in South Africa fizzled out.

The flame was rekindled in the early 'sixties and in 1962, the Great Britain team made a second tour to South Africa on their way home from Australia and New Zealand. Remarkably, they were not the only British tourists, as the crack Wakefield Trinity club also travelled to South Africa and played five games. Bizarrely, by this time, there were two rival organisations eager to promote Rugby League in South Africa and Fallowfield's diplomacy managed to keep both happy by ensuring both got a top-class touring team to visit them.

At the same time in 1962, another event took place in Ireland, this one organised by the Cloncliffe Harriers (an athletics club) and staged at the John F. Kennedy Stadium in Santry, County Dublin. Four top English clubs: Widnes, Workington Town, Featherstone Rovers and Huddersfield, were invited to play over the two days of Saturday 26th and Sunday 27th, May.

The Featherstone Rovers secretary at the time, Ron Bailey, recalls that the venue in Santry was an athletics stadium with just one large grandstand and elevated grass banking on the other three sides. On both days the stadium was well filled with estimated crowds of between 4,000 and 5,000 each day. Ron also remembers being asked to give a running commentary over the public-address system on both days, explaining the rules of the game to the audience as the play unfolded.

Nobody from the British Rugby League really knew too much about why the Cloncliffe Harriers came to promote a Rugby League tournament, but their official programme for the event expressed the hope that it would be *"the forerunner to many more such competitions."* They appeared to have substantial sponsorship support as the programme contained top quality full-page advertisments from companies like: Guinness, Aer Lingus airlines, the Irish Sweeps Derby and Cantrell and Cochrane's soft drinks of Dublin.

To some present day Rugby League followers it may seem incredible that the game had such a pioneering spirit of "going on the road" back then - around the same time in 1962 as the four clubs were travelling across the Irish sea and a fifth was going to South Africa, another two - local rivals Hull and Hull Kingston Rovers - were heading south-west to Cornwall where they played three exhibition matches in Penzance, Camborne and Falmouth. And all this activity was happening whilst the Great Britain team were on tour in Australia.

THE MAGNIFICENT CAREER OF TERRY CLAWSON

23 Years at the Top

Terry Clawson would probably have a chuckle at that headline, as some of the latter experiences of his long and illustrious career in Rugby League he would hardly rank at the top for a man who had known the pinnacle of being a World Cup winner. Certainly not the day he turned out for the last time, at the age of 40, playing for Hull in a miserable defeat up at Workington in April, 1980. That's the day when Terry got home he threw his boots in the dustbin and called it a day. It was 23 years on from the crisp late December afternoon in 1957 when the teenaged

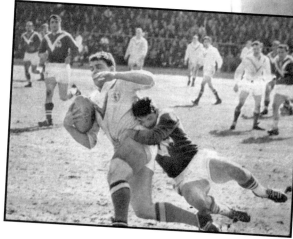

(Above) Terry in his days with York during 1974 and 1975.
(Left) The young Clawson playing in his second Test for Great Britain against France at the Gilbert Brutus Stadium in Perpignan in March, 1962. He had to wait ten years for another appearance for Great Britain which came, coincidentally, on the same pitch.

Clawson had entered the fray for the first time at Post Office Road as a Featherstone Rovers first-teamer - and started what turned out to be a magnificent career.

23 years and over 600 games is good going in anybody's language, but to do it as Terry did - at the coal-face of the forwards in the days when life in the scrums was no Sunday afternoon stroll - is even more special. In addition, Clawson had creative ball-handling skills and was a prolific goal-kicker. Wearing the old-style forward's boots, toe-end style, Terry kicked a grand total of 1,177 goals in his first class career. In those 23 seasons between 1957 and 1980, he played for nine different clubs (a couple of them in two different spells). For the record, Clawson's clubs were: Featherstone Rovers, Bradford Northern, Hull Kingston Rovers, Leeds, Oldham, York, Wakefield Trinity, Huddersfield and Hull. He will always be best associated with Featherstone in their great Cup fighting era, and then the Bradford Northern revival years of the 'sixties. Terry won 14 Great Britain caps, the first in 1962 and the last in 1974. After the disappointment of missing out on the 1962 tour, he finally achieved his ambition to be a Lion in Australia some twelve years later. In 1972 he was a key man in Great Britain's World Cup winning team. Such a great career deserved to be recorded in a fitting manner and Terry himself ensured it was - by writing one of the best sporting autobiographies ever published.

HALIFAX AND THE BATTLE OF two WELSH FULL-BACKS

(Above) GARFIELD OWEN saves the Halifax line as he tackles Wigan winger Frank Carlton in the 1961 Challenge Cup semi-final at a packed Station Road, Swinton.

(Above) RONNIE JAMES

Back in 1961 the streets of Halifax were simmering with heated opinions over who should wear the number one shirt in the famous blue and white hoops. The argument was over two Welshman and - to parody that well known saying about handbags - to have signed one outstanding goal-kicking full-back from the Principality was very fortunate; to have signed two was downright carelessness!

Garfield Owen was the man in possession. A fine player who had been outstanding for Halifax for the previous five years and was a big favourite with their supporters. But for two years in the "A" team, the younger Ronnie James had been biding his time and kicking his goals, waiting for his chance in the first team. When he got it, the controversy began over who should be the Halifax number one: Owen or James.

It was a sign of different times in Rugby League when Garfield Owen had gone north from Newport to join Halifax in 1956. He was the actual Welsh Rugby Union international full-back at the time and his signing - a huge media story - was broadcast live by BBC television. He made his debut in Albi, France, in a European Championship game and by the end of his first season in Rugby League was in the Great Britain shadow squad for the 1957 World Cup. But Halifax had always loved bringing Welshmen to Thrum Hall and, just three years after signing Garfield Owen, they signed another (less well known) full-back from Maesteg, called Ronnie James.

To some Halifax fans, it was unthinkable that such a pivotal and popular player as Garfield Owen be left out of their team. There were suggestions that both Welshmen should be accommodated in the side by James playing on the wing or at half-back. But, in the end, the Halifax board bit the bullet and decided to go for the younger man - allowing Owen to transfer to Keighley where he became a successful player-coach. Ronnie James never looked back and held the Halifax full-back role for over a decade.

They took Rugby League into everybody's home
PIONEERS OF BROADCASTING

Rugby League in the 21st Century is a sport very much dominated by Sky Television, whose myriad of commentators, interviewers, sideline-eyes and multi-camera intant replays, are a million miles away from the days when **Eddie Waring** *(pictured, right, in the commentary box)* was the face and voice of the game on television.

Eddie was the man who pioneered Rugby League on the telly. One of the game's great visionaries as a talented team manager, journalist and publicist, he did more than anybody to make the game known nationally on the B.B.C. - and Eddie would commentate alone on a full match without any co-commentators, assistants or action replays. The first national live broadcast of a Rugby League match was on 10th November, 1951 and was a Great Britain versus New Zealand Test match from Station Road, Swinton - although t.v. coverage of earlier Challenge Cup Finals had enjoyed limited reception in the south of England and the midlands.

Keith Macklin became a second familiar voice on both the television and radio coverage of Rugby League. *(Pictured, left)* we see a young Macklin conducting a very rare filmed interview for television with the legendary try-scorer Brian Bevan at Wilderspool, Warrington. Keith first did radio commentary in 1956 and went on to complete a marvellous half-century of broadcasting - and is still going strong.

The very first radio broadcast on the game was by the B.B.C. on 7th May, 1927, and was on the Challenge Cup Final between Oldham and Swinton played at Wigan. And in the days before the advent of local radio, the BBC Home Service in the north of England would provide regular round-ups of results and reports every Saturday evening. One of their best known commentators was Yorkshireman **George Potts.** *(Pictured, right)* George is conducting an interview with the Featherstone Rovers Chairman Mr.Bob Jackson at Post Office Road during a "Spotlight on Featherstone Rovers" programme for the B.B.C. North's *"Sporting Diary"* in November, 1957. Other Featherstone personalities in the gorup are, left to right: Abe Bullock (President), Ron Bailey (Secretary), John Jepson (Vice-chairman) and Bessie Major (of the Ladies committee.)

Remember when

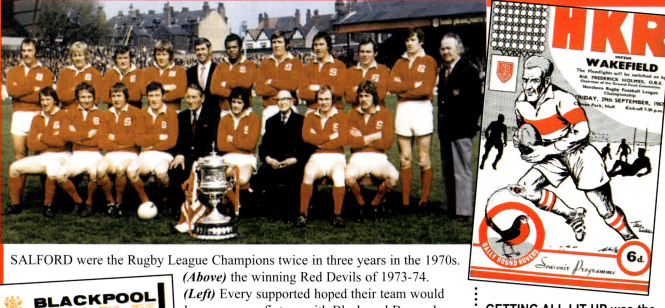

SALFORD were the Rugby League Champions twice in three years in the 1970s. *(Above)* the winning Red Devils of 1973-74.
(Left) Every supported hoped their team would have an away fixture with Blackpool Borough during the illuminations, as Oldham did in 1965.
(Below, right) John Woods led Leigh to the Championship in 1980-81 and this photo shows the Leigh maestro in action against Warrington.
(Below) Bob Haigh of Leeds set a new tries-in-a-season record by a forward when he scored 40 in 1970-71. Here's the 37th of those tries which actually broke the record, it was versus Batley at Headingley.

GETTING ALL LIT UP was the new trend in the 1960s as Floodlit Rugby League caught on. *(Above)* the match when Hull K.R. switched on their new floodlights in 1967.

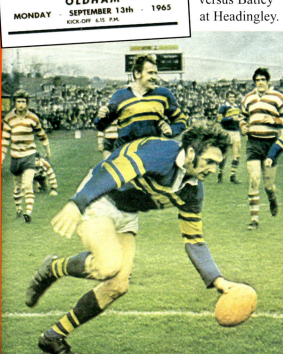

PHOTO by EDDIE WHITHAM

AN EVER-PRESENT IN THE HISTORY OF SUPER LEAGUE

SENIOR'S SERVICE
Sheffield, Leeds & Great Britain

PHOTO by ANDREW VARLEY PICTURE AGENCY

Keith Senior is the only current player in the Super League who can claim to have been there right from the very start. The big centre has made his reputation as a key member of the Leeds title-winning teams of more recent years, but Senior was in the line-up for Sheffield Eagles on that famous night in Paris in March, 1996, when Super League was launched.

It was a magical occasion at the Charlety Stadium as over 17,000 fans roared Paris Saint Germain home to an emotional victory as they kicked off the brave new world of European Rugby League. Senior and the Eagles were beaten that night, but two years later were to enjoy a glorious victory in the Challenge Cup Final, beating hot favourites Wigan in one of the biggest upsets ever seen at Wembley.

When Sheffield Eagles founder Gary Hetherington moved to Leeds, he wasted little time in making Keith Senior one of his first major signings and, ever since, Headingley crowds have enjoyed the power-packed performances of one of the modern game's top centres. Fast forward 12 years from that opening night in Paris in 1996, and 31-years-old Keith kicked off the 2008 season holding the record for Super League appearances and tries - 155 tries in 303 games - and has continued to add to that throughout this year's campaign.

With 33 Test appearances for Great Britain he stands sixth in the all-time list of most capped players - a marvellous achievement for the lad who hails from Huddersfield and began his junior rugby with the Milnsbridge Amateur club. When the talk is of Super League survivors, nobody has given longer service than Senior.

A reminder of another age at Headingley as the "Leeds Loiner" official programme welcomed fans on Saturday afternoons - an era of favourites like Lewis Jones, Jeff Stevenson, Derek Hallas and company.

44

CLUB NOSTALGIA

(Pictured) GUS RISMAN carries the Challenge Cup for Workington Town at Wembley in 1952. Behind captain Gus is Billy Ivison, followed down the famous 39 steps of Wembley by Tony Paskins. It was Workington's finest hour.

In the following section we present a page of memories and nostlagia on all the favourite clubs you grew up with . . .

Club Nostalgia - BARROW

The Barrow team in 1966-67 pictured at Craven Park wearing a white "change" kit rather than the familiar blue with white vee - by the end of the season they were at Wembley. Left to right, *(Standing):* Keith Irving, Terry Kirchin, Brian Backhouse, Ray Hopwood, Maurice Redhead, Ivor Kelland, Mick Watson, Jim Challinor (player-coach).
(In front): Harry Hughes, Bill Burgess, Tom Brophy, Eddie Tees, Tommy Dawes, Ged Smith and Bob Wear.

Five Star Favourites

*WILLIE HORNE
Barrow's ultimate legend and greatest player - in 1955 he led them to the Cup at Wembley. See his statue outside Craven Park.

*BILL BURGESS
A Test player and Lions tourist like his father, a brilliant winger of the '60s

*EDDIE SZYMALA
Rough and tough, enforcer Eddie was a massive favourite at Craven Park.

*DAVID CAIRNS
Smart scrum-half from Askam who won Lancs. Cup in 1983 and played for Great Britain in 1984.

*DARREN HOLT
Present-day Barrow loyal servant who broke Willie Horne's goals record.

(Above) Programme for a 1971 tour match that turned out to be a thriller, won 25-15 by the Kiwis.

DO YOU KNOW?
Which club came in and paid a big transfer fee to get Bill Burgess to join them?

(Above) At Wembley in 1957, Barrow's third Challenge Cup Final in six years, Willie Horne introduces his team to the Earl of Derby.

Club Nostalgia - BATLEY

The Batley team in 1963 before playing at Wakefield at Belle Vue, and including the future famous coach Peter Fox. Left to right: *(Standing):* J.Briggs, D.Fairbanks, J.Fryer, E.Illingworth, L.Johnston, P.Fox, P.McVeigh. *(In front):* J.Ireland, D.Foster, J.Lawton, I.Geldard, M.Shuttleworth and M.Hammond.

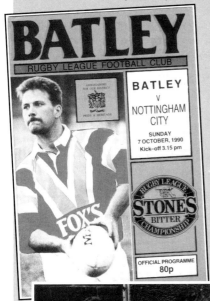

(Right) Glen Tomlinson, in action for Batley as they went so close to promotion in 1993-94.

(Below) Three favourites of the Gallant Youths at Mount Pleasant in the early 1950s: Bill Riches, John Etty and Doug Stokes.

Five Star Favourites

*JOHN ETTY
Batley's best known rugby product - star winger for Yorkshire county, John later played for Oldham and Wakefield Trinity.

*TREVOR WALKER
"Tank" set a record for tries scored by an open-side prop forward.

*CARL GIBSON
Batley Boys product who became the last Gallant Youth to play in a Test match for Great Britain in 1985 - later signed for Leeds for £50,000.

*GLEN TOMLINSON
Aussie half-back of the early 1990s, so popular at Mount Pleasant they named a stand after him.

*PAUL STOREY
Gave over a decade of fine service to Batley as their full-back, and later became the club coach.

DO YOU KNOW?

Which future Warrington and England international second-row forward began his professional Rugby League career with Batley?

Club Nostalgia - BLACKPOOL

Blackpool Borough, captained by a young scrum-half called Tommy Bishop, pictured in August, 1962 at their old St.Annes Road Stadium, before playing against Workington Town. Left to right: *(Standing):* Wilkshire, Givvons, Collingwood, Abram, Normington, Hopwood. *(Seated):* Hooper, Gee, Pimblett, Bishop, Bowden, Molloy and Clayton.

Five Star Favourites

*TOMMY BISHOP
The Borough's most famous product. Starred at Blackpool in the early 'sixties and became the world's top scrum-half.

*TEX McCARRICK
Big goal-kicking full-back of the 1960s, set a point-scoring record for Blackpool Borough.

*JIMMY JOHNSON
Top try-scoring winger who was a seaside favourite in the early '70s.

*JIMMY HAMILTON
Very talented prop in the side that reached the John Player Trophy Final in 1977, Cumbria county player and a real stalwart of the Blackpool club.

*JIM MOLYNEUX
A Wiganer who gave great service to Blackpool through the 1970s and '80s, first man to win the Kilkenny trophy three times.

(Above) ROGER DUFTY in action for Blackpool versus Warrington in 1967 at Borough Park with Brian Holmes and Alan Whitworth in support.

(Left) PAUL GAMBLE - local boy who became one of Blackpool's longest serving players.

(Left) BRIAN WINSTANLEY receives the Blackpool player-of-the-year award for 1966-67 from the donor of the handsome trophy, Mr. Joe Kilkenny.

DO YOU KNOW?

Who was the American winger who played for Blackpool in the 1960s?

Club Nostalgia - BRADFORD

(Above) The Bradford Northern team in 1972-73, a Wembley year for them. Left to right, *(Back row):* Brian Hogan, Kel Earl, Stan Fearnley, Bill Pattinson, Stuart Carlton. Arnie Long, Stuart Gallacher. *(Middle row):* Graham Joyce, Phil Doyle, Lewis Cardiss, Peter Dunn, Dave Stockwell, Peter Small. *(Front row):* Bak Diabira, David Treasure, Mick Blacker, Eddie Tees (captain), Dave Redfearn, Mike Lamb and Barry Seabourne.

(Right) Cartoonist's impression of the Odsal maestro TOMMY SMALES in the 1960s.

(Above) 1967 action at Odsal Stadium as Bradford loose-forward JOHNNY RAE and scrum-half BAK DIABIRA get stuck into a Leeds opponent

(Above) KEITH MUMBY one of the longest serving players in the history of the Bradford club.

DO YOU KNOW?

Which two Bradford Northern players captained Great Britain in consecutive years?

Five Star Favourites

*ERNEST WARD
Imposing figure as the captain of Bradford in three successive Wembley Finals.

*TOMMY SMALES
The creative genius who moulded the Bradford revival of the mid-1960s.

*KEITH MUMBY
Rock solid full-back who played 588 games for Bradford - more than any other player.

*KARL FAIRBANK
"Konkreet" was a farmer who won 16 Test caps and was the dynamo of the Odsal pack

*ROBBIE PAUL
Came as a teenager from New Zealand and became the talisman figure of the Bulls' Super League era.

Club Nostalgia - BRAMLEY

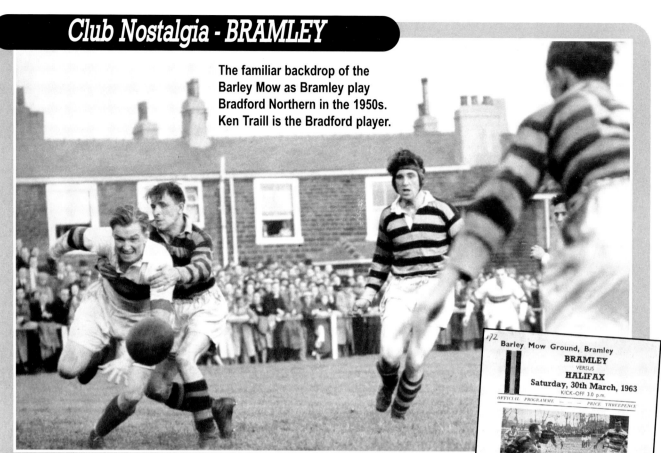

The familiar backdrop of the Barley Mow as Bramley play Bradford Northern in the 1950s. Ken Traill is the Bradford player.

Five Star Favourites

*DAVE HORN
Local lad whose family were steeped in Bramley's history - the big prop gave 13 years loyal service.

*JOHN WOLFORD
Probably Bramley's best ever player, brilliant footballer played 14 seasons for the Villagers.

*ARTHUR KEEGAN
Ex-Test full-back was player-coach as Bramley won their only major cup, the BBC Floodlit Trophy in 1973 - a real gentleman.

*JACK AUSTIN
"Fiery Jack" was a big inspiration from the wing in that famous Floodlit Trophy run to glory.

* PETER LISTER
Very talented attacker throughout the 1980s, who set a club try-scoring record in 1985-86.

(Above) Bramley favourite JOHN WOLFORD dives over to score in a famous win by the Villagers over big city neighbours Leeds at Headingley.

DO YOU KNOW?

Which well known Leeds bookmaker was a high profile supporter of Bramley?

(Left) Bramley with some well known names in 1985. Left to right, *(Standing)*: Pitchford, Lister, Lean, Clarkson, Bullough, Harrison, Gascoigne, Bowman.
(In front): Lund, Beale, Kelly, Fletcher (captain), Dyas, Kilner and Mason.

Club Nostalgia - CASTLEFORD

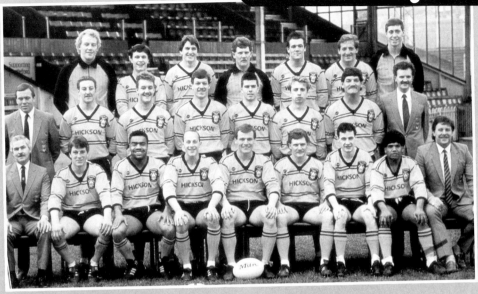

Castleford, the Cup winners in 1986. Left to right: *(Back row):* Alan Shillito, Roy Southernwood, Barry Johnson, Kevin Beardmore, Keith England, Ian Fletcher, Neil Battye. *(Middle row):* Malcom Reilly (coach), Keith Jones, Dean Mountain, Gary Hyde, Phil Payne, Neil Greatbatch, Kevin Ward, Stuart Walker (physio). *(Front row):* Mr. David Poulter (chairman), Stuart Horton, David Plange, Tony Marchant, John Joyner (captain), Bob Beardmore, David Roockley, Jamie Sandy, Dave Sampson ("A" team coach).

(Above) ALBERT LUNN Goal-kicking full-back who is a big part of the history of Castleford.

DO YOU KNOW?

Can you name four Castleford players who joined the Manly club to play in Australia?

(Right) **Happiness at Wembley in 1969 for scrum-half Keith Hepworth and goal-kicking second-row forward Mick Redfearn, after Castleford had beaten Salford to take the Challenge Cup back to Wheldon Road. They were back the following year to beat Wigan and retain the Cup.**

Five Star Favourites

*JOHN SHERIDAN
A wonderful servant to Cas' as a 300-game player, 1955 to 1966, and then a coach and mentor.

*ALAN HARDISTY
Most brilliant Castleford star of them all - helped earn the "Classy Cas" tag.

* KEITH HEPWORTH
Other half of the famous partnership with Hardisty. Toughest of scrum-halves.

*MALCOLM REILLY
Swashbuckling figure in the Wembley teams and later brought great success to Castleford as coach.

*JOHN JOYNER
Played more games for the club and won more Test caps than any other Castleford player.

(Left) **A fly-on-the-wall view inside the Castleford dressing room in the late 1960s as skipper Alan Hardisty and young half-back Danny Hargrave focus on the game they were about to go out and play.**

Club Nostalgia - DEWSBURY

Dewsbury as the reigning Rugby League Champions in 1973-74, pictured before playing at Wigan. Left to right, *(Standing):* John Maloney, John Bates, Graham Chalkley, Trevor Lowe, Harry Beverley, Jeff Grayshon, Keith Voyce, Steve Hankins. *(In front):* Nigel Stephenson, Greg Ashcroft, Alan Bates, Alan Agar, Adrian Rushton, Terry Day and Garry Mitchell.

Five Star Favourites

*HARRY HAMMOND
Mighty prop was a rock for Dewsbury in the first post-War decade - played for Yorkshire.

*ALVYN NEWALL
Scrum-half and captain through the 1960s, he led Dewsbury to two Challenge Cup semi-finals.

*MIKE STEPHENSON
Dewsbury's best known player and captain of the 1973 Championship winning team. A World Cup winner in 1972.

*DON RICHARDSON
A scrum-half as an amateur who moved to full-back and was very loyal to Dewsbury, playing 256 games between 1976 and 1988.

*CHRIS VASEY
Talented stand-off who played six years at Crown Flatt before being transferred to Leeds in 1988-89 for a record fee.

(Above) DENNIS BAILEY - 1980s Dewsbury winger.

DO YOU KNOW?

Which brothers from Dewsbury went on the 1974 Lions tour to Australia?

Mike Stephenson leads the attack against Wakefield at Crown Flatt in the Dewsbury Championship-winning year of 1973, with namesake Nigel in support.

Club Nostalgia - DONCASTER

Doncaster at Tatters Field in the 1975-76 season. Left to right, *(Standing):* Larry Lester, Eric Broom, John Green, Graham Arrand, Maurice Pearson, Malcolm Yates, Chris Stenton, Terry Lawrence, Keith Tomlinson.
(In front): Trevor Denton, Ken Rushton, David Varey, Peter Bell, Alan Goodyear and Graham Guy.

(Left) GARETH PRICE pictured as the Doncaster club's very first captain coach as they entered the Rugby League in 1951. The Welshman had signed from Halifax.

Two great Dons favourites - *(Above)* AUDLEY PENNANT in the 1994 promotion winning team, and *(Left)* GRAHAM ARRAND a hero of the battling years of the 1960s.

DO YOU KNOW?

Who coached Doncaster when they won promotion in 1994?

Five Star Favourites

*PETER GOODCHILD
Top class wingman in the 1960s, became the first Doncaster player to be selected for Yorkshire.

*GRAHAM ARRAND
Local boy who gave loyal service as powerful three-quarter in the '60s and '70s - also played in Australia for North Sydney.

*TONY BANHAM
The "Cockney Rebel" was a big prop who proved unstoppable near the line - similar to a future Dons favouite Kevin Parkhouse.

*DAVID NOBLE
Incredibly loyal and durable player who scored a record 1751 points for Doncaster between 1976 and 1992.

*MARK ROACHE
Set a Dons career record of 111 tries in 11 seasons with the club - this winger was always very popular with the Doncaster fans.

Club Nostalgia - FEATHERSTONE

(Right) Featherstone Rovers the famous Cup fighters, pictured at Station Road, Swinton on 19th March, 1960, before beating the home side 11-7 in the Challenge Cup quarter-final. The Rovers players are, left to right, *(Standing):* Joe Anderson, Terry Clawson, Malcolm Dixon, Frank Smith, Colin Clift, Cliff Lambert. *(In front):* Jack Fennell, Don Fox, Ken Greatorex, Joe Mullaney (captain), Willis Fawley, Jim Hunt and Cyril Woolford.

Five Star Favourites

*TERRY CLAWSON
One of Rugby League's great characters and best all-round forwards. Began his remarkable 23-year career at Rovers.

*MALCOLM DIXON
Big forward who led Featherstone to their first Wembley win in 1967 and won Test honours.

*DON FOX
Natural footballer and much loved Rovers favourite - 12 seasons at Post Office Road. Big for a scrum-half he eventually moved up t the pack.

*JIMMY THOMPSON
Fame for his text-book tackling, second-rower Jimmy was a Cup-winner at Wembley in 1967 and an Ashes winner in 1970.

*STEVE NASH
One of Brtain's best scrum-halves, won the Lance Todd Trophy with Featherstone in 1973 and was a World Cup winner in 1972.

Memories of those Wembley triumphs for Featherstone.
(Above, left) Second-rowers Arnold Morgan and Jimmy Thompson do a lap of honour with the Cup in 1967.
(Left) Cyril Kellett kicking one of his eight goals as Rovers regained the Cup in 1973.

DO YOU KNOW?

Who kicked the winning goal last time Featherstone won a Cup Final at Wembley - and which club had he signed for the Rovers from?

Club Nostalgia - HALIFAX

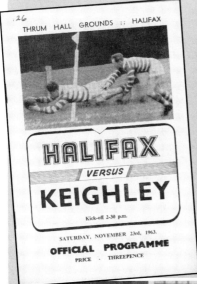

(Above) Joy for Chris Anderson and his Halifax team - the Challenge Cup winners at Wembley in 1987.

(Above) Halifax's favourite try-scorer Johnny Freeman chaired by team-mates on the occasion of his benefit match at Thrum Hall against Keighley in the 166-67 season. The other players are: Ian Foye, John Burnett, Colin Dixon, Barrie Cooper and Charlie Renilson.

(Above) JACK WILKINSON prop-forward in the feared Halifax pack of the 1950s.

Champions! Halifax players Paul Dixon and Scott Wilson show their delight at winning the Rugby League Championship trophy at the end of the 1985-86 season - glory days at Thrum Hall.

Five Star Favourites

*JOHNNY FREEMAN
Came from Cardiff to bcome a Halifax legend. Scored 290 tries in 396 games in a 13-year career at Thrum Hall.

*RONNIE JAMES
Welsh full-back from Maesteg was the first Halifax player to kick more than 1,000 goals.

*ALAN KELLETT
Ovenden lad who could not stay away for long from Halifax in a 17-year playing career.

*CHARLIE RENILSON
Scotsman who played 12 years at loose-forward for 'Fax - starring in the 1965 Championship win and representing Gt.Britain.

*PAUL DIXON
A farmer from Underbank who was a tower of strength in the pack as Championship and Cup were won in the 1980s.

DO YOU KNOW?

Who dropped a goal to help Halifax to a one point win over St.Helens in the 1987 Cup Final at Wembley?

Club Nostalgia - HARLEQUINS

When it seemed like the London Broncos were going to take over the world in 1997 as Richard Branson gave his backing to the capital city club. *(Above)* Mr. Branson packs down alongside Martin Offiah and several Broncos' young hopefuls. *(Right)* Terry Matterson on the front cover of the programme for the battle of the Broncos between London and Brisbane in the 1997 World Club Championship.

Five Star Favourites

*REG BOWDEN
Player-coach and leader of the original Fulham club as the first seeds were sown in London.

*HUSSEIN M'BARKI
Moroccan winger was their first exotic discovery and he played a big part in R.L. in London.

*FRANK FEIGHAN
A genuine London Rugby League hero, starred during the turbulent 1980s years at Chiswick.

*TULSEN TOLLETT
Gave long service in the Broncos era, and always a good ambassador.

*ROBERT PURDHAM
Longest serving player as the Broncos became Harlequins, captained club and country and a model professional since signing from Whitehaven.

(Above) REG BOWDEN - as player-coach of the original Fulham club in 1980, as Rugby League in London enjoyed such joyous times.

(Above) ROBERT PURDHAM - Cumbrian captain of Harlequins.

DO YOU KNOW?

Where was the home ground of the London Broncos in the first Super League season of 1996?

Club Nostalgia - HUDDERSFIELD

A reminder of the industrial landscape of the north as the champion Huddersfield team lined up before playing Hunslet at Parkside in March, 1949. The players are, left to right, *(Standing):* George Wilson, J.L.Davies, Russ Pepperell, John Daly, Ike Owens, A.Ferguson, S.Lightfoot, Lionel Cooper, Jeff Bawden. *(In front):* Johnny Hunter, Jock Anderson, Pat Devery (captain), Bob Nicholson, Billy Banks and Dave Valentine.

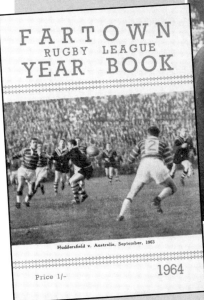

(Above) Huddersfield captain Tommy Smales introduces full-back Frank Dyson to Lord Derby before the 1962 Championship Final, as Fartown teammates Harry Deighton and Aiden Breen look on.

(Above) No town has such a fine tradition for producing top quality Rugby League literature as Huddersfield, including many years of the "Fartown Yearbook."

DO YOU KNOW?
Who played for Huddersfield in both the 1953 and 1962 Challenge Cup Finals?

(Left) LIONEL COOPER the big winger from Australia who will always remain one of the great legends of Fartown. He scored 420 tries in 333 games for Huddersfield.

Five Star Favourites

*JOHNNY HUNTER
Came to Fartown as Lionel Cooper's travelling partner, and 10 years later was a cult figure.

*DAVE VALENTINE
The Great Scot, captained Huddersfield and carved a World Cup legend for Britain in 1954.

*MICK SULLIVAN
Signed for Fartown as a junior in 1952 and five years later left for the game's record transfer-fee. Became his country's most capped player.

*KEN SENIOR
Played 17 years for the club and represented Great Britain - done much to preserve the claret and gold traditions.

*TREVOR LEATHLEY
Loyal player for 13 years through the tough times of the 1970s and '80s

Club Nostalgia - HULL

Roy Francis & the Boulevard boys

One of the game's pivotal coaches, Roy Francis, pictured at the Boulevard with his Hull team of 1959-60, including players like: Johnny Whiteley (captain), Bill Drake, Brian Saville, Mick Scott, Peter Bateson, Sam Evans, Jim Drake, Nan Halafihi, Stan Cowan and Tommy Harris. And yes, that is a clipboard Roy is holding!

Five Star Favourites

*JOHNNY WHITELEY
"Mr.Hull" - Johnny led the "Airlie Birds" twice at Wembley and played 417 games for the club.

*TOMMY HARRIS
Welsh hooker at the Boulevard throughout the 1950s, an all-time great.

*CLIVE SULLIVAN
Much admired World Cup captain, scored a record 250 tries for Hull

*STEVE NORTON
Signed from Castleford and was the creative genius in the triumphs of the late 1970s / early '80s.

*MICK CRANE
One of Hull's favourite local boys, broke all the rules on fitness, but a natural footballer who played 324 Hull games.

(Above) Hull F.C. half-backs Tony Dean and David Topliss lift the Yorkshire Cup after victory in the 1983-84 season Final against Castleford at Elland Road, Leeds. The "Airlie Birds" won that Final 13-2 in what was the middle of a trio of consecutive Hull wins of a famous and handsome old trophy - once one of the celebrated "All Four Cups."

(Above) Programme from a Challenge Cup-tie derby in 1972.

DO YOU KNOW?

Which Hull player won the Lance Todd trophy in the 1960 Challenge Cup Final?

Club Nostalgia - HULL K. R.

Hull Kingston Rovers at the start of the 1971-72 season in which they qualified for the Yorkshire Cup Final and eventually beat Castleford 11-7. The players are: left to right, *(Standing):* John Moore, Terry Clawson, Steve Wiley, George Kirkpatrick, Cliff Wallis, Eric Palmer, Phil Coupland, Paul Rose. *(In front):* Paul Daley, Mike Stephenson, Paul Longstaff, Roger Millward (captain), Peter "Flash" Flanagan, Colin Cooper and Ian Markham.

(Left) Alan Burwell and Harry Poole in the 1964-65 season when both were chosen to captain Great Britain, at Under-24 and full Test levels respectively, only for injury to rule both out.

DO YOU KNOW?
Which Hull K.R. player was in the Great Britain team as they won the 1972 World Cup Final?

(Right) Hull Kingston Rovers at Wembley for the first time in 1964 - as prop Brian Tyson attempts to beat the Widnes defence. In support is the young forward Brian Mennell who made his Robins first team debut in this Cup Final.

Five Star Favourites

*HARRY POOLE
The captain who, more than anybody, turned the Robins into a force in the game in the 1960s. Led them to their first Wembley Final in 1964.

*GRAHAM PAUL
"The Cornish Express" was a crowd-pleaser who scored 116 tries in 197 games.

*PETER FLANAGAN
"Flash" embodied the spirit of the Robins in the swinging sixties - and won 14 Great Britain Test caps.

*ROGER MILLWARD
The little genius who gave marvellous service as both player and coach. Played 406 games for Hull K.R. and is one of the game's greats.

*PHIL LOWE
A name synonymous with Hull K.R. - a teenage giant who went on to be one of the world's best forwards.

Club Nostalgia - HUNSLET

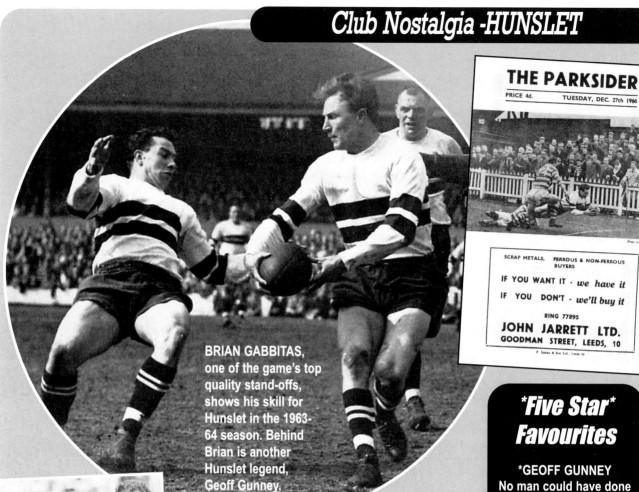

BRIAN GABBITAS, one of the game's top quality stand-offs, shows his skill for Hunslet in the 1963-64 season. Behind Brian is another Hunslet legend, Geoff Gunney.

(Above) GRAHAM KING, tough Hunslet scrum-half as they won promotion in 1987.

(Above) Hunslet line up early in the 1962-63 season without four of their biggest names - Brian Gabbitas, Geoff Gunney, Bernard Prior and Fred Ward - who were all away on representative duties. The players pictured are, left to right, (Standing): Barry Lee, Bill Ramsey, K.Whitehead, Billy Langton, Ken Eyre, Sam Smith, Dennis Hartley. (In front): M.Garforth, Alan Preece, Geoff Shelton, Jeff Stevenson, Willie Walker and I.Robinson. It proved to be a good season at Parkside, as Hunslet won the Yorkshire Cup and also the Division Two championsip to clinch promotion.

DO YOU KNOW?

Who captained Hunslet at Wembley in the 1965 Challenge Cup Final?

Five Star Favourites

*GEOFF GUNNEY
No man could have done more for his local club than Geoff - played over 600 games in a 22-year career between 1951 and 1973, and then saved the club from closure.

*BRIAN GABBITAS
Another of the top class players at Parkside, he starred for Hunslet in the 1965 Wembley Final.

*BILLY LANGTON
Goal-kicking full-back who scored in every match in 1958-59 as Hunslet finished as runners-up in the Championship Final.

*BILL RAMSEY
Talented second-row who played at Wembley in 1965 and was a Lions tourist in 1966.

*KENNY SYKES
Loyal as they come, York lad Kenny played in the last team at Parkside in 1973 and then was part of the New Hunslet revival.

Club Nostalgia - KEIGHLEY

Keighley pictured at a snowy Lawkholme Lane in 1967 - among the familiar faces on the front row are captain Alan Kellett, star full-back Brian Jefferson and Welsh scrum-half Colin Evans. Among the forwards at the back, long-serving loose-forward Bill Aspinall and ex-Hull Kingston Rovers forager Keith Pollard.

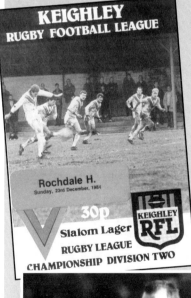

(Right) BRYAN TODD in Keighley days back in the early 1960s. "Toddy" was a top centre, who also played for Halifax and St.Helens, representing Yorkshire County, before emigrating to Australia.
(Below) BRENDAN HILL in action at the time Keighley was going "Cougar-crazy" in the 1990s. The mighty prop truly was a *big* favourite with the fans.

Five Star Favourites

*TERRY HOLLINDRAKE
The only Keighley born player to play in a Test for Great Britain - big winger with the famous sidestep.

*ROY SABINE
Classy stand-off played 175 games for Keighley and represented Yorkshire, and later coached Keighley to a Cup semi-final.

*BRIAN JEFFERSON
Keighley's points-scoring record breaker - 2,116 points in a 13-season career. Played for England.

*PETER ROE
Local boy who gave great service at Lawkholme, first as a strapping young centre and later as a successful coach.

*MARTIN WOOD
Skilful footballer who was such an influential figure in the successes of the Cougar years.

DO YOU KNOW?

Which Amateur club did Keighley sign Terry Hollindrake from?

Club Nostalgia - LEEDS

(Above) The Loiners team who won the Rugby League Championship in the 1968-69 season. Left to right, *(Standing):* John Langley, Ray Batten, Tony Crosby, Mick Clark, Albert Eyre, Bill Ramsey, David Hick, John Atkinson, Ken Eyre. *(Seated):* Alan Smith, Syd Hynes, Bernard Watson, Joe Warham (manager-coach) Barry Seabourne (captain), Mr.Jack Myerscough (football chairman), Bev Risman, Ron Cowan and Mick Shoebottom.

Five Star Favourites

*LEWIS JONES Perhaps the ultimate Welsh "golden boy," signed for Leeds in 1952 and became a legend in the city.

*JOHN ATKINSON Class winger as half of great double act with Alan Smith - "Atky" scored 340 tries for Leeds.

*MICK SHOEBOTTOM Never a more popular Loiner, the great hearted stand-off cruelly struck down by injury in 1971.

*JOHN HOLMES Brilliant all-rounder, Kirkstall boy who played more games than anybody else for Leeds in 23 years at Headingley.

*KEVIN SINFIELD Leader of the modern day Leeds for a decade, a very creative footballer signed as an Oldham schoolboy.

(Above) SYD HYNES lifts another trophy for Leeds with team-mates Graham Eccles, Phil Cookson, John Holmes and David Ward mixing with young fans.

Famous wing-threequarters who wore the blue and amber with distinction.
(Above) WILF ROSENBERG, the "Flying Dentist" from South Africa in 1960-61.
(Left) ALAN SMITH, scoring one of his 283 tries for Leeds in a 21-year career.

DO YOU KNOW?

Which Leeds player won the Lance Todd Trophy in 1977?

Club Nostalgia - LEIGH

(Above) Leigh in the 1963-64 season, a line-up that includes their former England R.U. stand-off Bev Risman and mighty forwards Bill Robinson and Stan Owen.

(Above) MICK MARTYN, with familiar scrum-cap, in action for Leigh against Blackpool Borough at the St.Anne's Road Stadium.

(Above) MICK STACEY - a prolific points scorer for Leigh, signed in 1971 and loyal to the club for over a decade.

DO YOU KNOW?

Who were the two Australian Rugby Union internationals who joined Leigh in the early 1950s?

Five Star Favourites

*MICK MARTYN
From a great Leigh family of Rugby League players, Mick was a prolific try-scorer for a forward. Went on the famous 1958 tour.

*MICK COLLINS
Played 408 games for Leigh as a stylish centre, capped by the Wembley victory of 1971.

*ROD TICKLE
One of the game's fastest wingers, he thrilled the Hilton Park crowds for a decade, scoring 114 tries.

*JOHN WOODS
Probably the most talented footballer to come out of Leigh. A key part of the 1981-82 Championship.

*DES DRUMMOND
One of Britain's most explosive wingers, with Woods, he helped put Leigh on the R.L. map.

Club Nostalgia - LIVERPOOL

As Huyton, pictured at Alt Park in the 1974-75 season. Left to right, *(Standing)*: Graham Walshaw, Don Parry, Brian Grady, Terry Hammil, Les Westhead, Norman Williams, Derek Watts, Geoff Smart (coach), G.Burrows (physio). *(In front):* Doug Davies, John Evans, Allan Nuttall, Dave Leatherbarrow, Terry Gorman (captain), Keith Wills, Trevor Lloyd and Robin Whitfield.

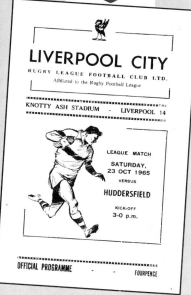

Five Star Favourites

*WILF HUNT
Goal-kicker who was always first on the score-sheet for Liverpool City at Knotty Ash during the 1950s and early '60s

*RAY ASHBY
Talented running full-back who represented Great Britain in 1964 as a Liverpool City player.

*TERRY GORMAN
Experienced scrum-half who had begun his pro' career with Huddersfield in the 1950s, did a good job as Huyton player-coach in the mid-1970s.

*KEITH WILLS
Excellent loose-forward who represented Lancashire County as a Huyton player.

*GEOFF FLETCHER
From prop-forward to chairman. Kept the club going all the way from Huyton to Highfield.

(Above) LES HOCKENHULL, a great stalwart during the Knotty Ash days, pictured with his Liverpool City team-mates receiving a presentation to mark his Testimonial.
(Left) As Runcorn Highfield, Danny Campbell, Steve Simm and Arthur Daley are this trio of players during the era the club played at Canal Street.

DO YOU KNOW?

What were the traditional colours of the Liverpool City team in the 1950s and '60s?

Club Nostalgia - OLDHAM

Oldham pictured at Watersheddings at the start of the 1972-73 season. Left to right, *(Back row):* Cliff Hill, Bill Churm, Keith Ashcroft, Norman Hodgkinson, Ken "Tug" Wilson, Arthur Daley, Geoff Munro, Graham Starkey (coach). *(Middle row):* Kevin Taylor, Jim Reynolds, Phil Larder, Frank Foster (captain), Keith Jackson, Mike Elliott. *(In front):* Mick McCone, Johnny Blair, Martin Murphy, Mick Siddall and Tom Davies.

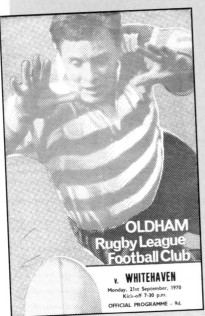

Two Yorkshiremen in the back division of the very successful Oldham team of the mid-1950s. *(Right)* DICK CRACKNELL, an England international winger from Huddersfield and *(below)* JOHN ETTY, powerful winger signed from Batley, pictured on his way to a try against Warrington.

Five Star Favourites

*BERNARD GANLEY
The goal-kicking full-back of the great 1950s side. Kicked 1,358 goals in 341 Oldham games.

*FRANK PITCHFORD
Brilliant scrum-half in the 1957 Championship team, toured with the 1958 Lions.

*ALAN DAVIES
One of the finest centres in the game, another 1957 title winner. He set a club try-scoring record of 174.

*MARTIN MURPHY
Full-back who played a massive 462 games for Oldham in a 16-year career from 1966 to 1982.

*TERRY FLANAGAN
Local from Saddleworth, loose-forward whose skills won Test honours and led Oldham from 1979 to '89.

DO YOU KNOW?

Who was Oldham's coach when they won the Northern Rugby League Championship in 1957, and who did they beat in the Final?

Club Nostalgia - ROCHDALE

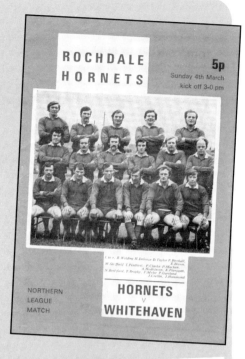

Rochdale Hornets pictured at the Athletic Grounds in 1973. Left to right, (Back row): Tony Halmshaw, Henry Delooze, Bob Welding, Bill Holliday, Peter Birchall, Alan Hodkinson. (Middle row): Bill Sheffield, Jim Crellin, Norman Brelsford, Peter Clarke, Willie Aspinall, Rod Tickle. (Front row): Stuart Whitehead, Tom Brophy, Peter Gartland, John Butler, John Hammond and Ray Harris.

Five Star Favourites

*TED CAHILL
Hornets full-back throughout the 1950s. A native of St.Helens, Ted played for England and was a 1954 Lions tourist.

*JOHNNY FISHWICK
Scrum-half with all the skills in the late 1950s and early '60s.

*JOE CHAMBERLAIN
Full-back who hailed from Warrington and gave a decade of loyal service to Rochdale.

*GRAHAM STARKEY
Smart player during the 1960s, became Hornets player-coach and, later, one of Rugby League's coaching mentors.

*NORMAN BRELSFORD
Nippy and elusive winger who entertained the Hornets fans with years of tries.

(Right) TED CAHILL
The Rochdale full-back who toured Australia with the 1954 Great Britain team -signed from Liverpool, he had learned his rugby with the Vine Tavern junior club.

(Above) JOE CHAMBERLAIN in action for Rochdale in 1970. Joe was one of the most dedicated players ever to wear the Hornets red, white and blue colours - he later became a referee.

(Above) BILL HOLLIDAY leads Rochdale Hornets out for the 1973-74 "Players No.6 Trophy" Final against Warrington at Wigan. He is followed immediately by Hornets winger NORMAN BRELSFORD who scored two tries in a 27-16 defeat for Rochdale.

DO YOU KNOW?

Who was the Rochdale Hornets coach when they reached the "Players No.6 Trophy" Final in 1973-74.

Club Nostalgia - SALFORD

(Left) The Red Devils of Salford in 1970, with the club's influential chairman, Mr. Brian Snape, standing on the right of the group. He inspired the great Reds revival of that era.

(Right) Salford had six players selected for the 1975 World Championships in Australia - three for England and three for Wales. Here, the magnificent six line up on picture day at the Willows: Mike Coulman, Colin Dixon, David Watkins, Ken Gill, Peter Banner and Keith Fielding.

(Left) ERIC PRESCOTT was a big money signing by Salford in 1972 from St.Helens. Tough tackling Eric went on to play 12 seasons for the Reds.

(Above) MARTIN DICKENS and JACKIE BRENNAN, pictured in training for the 1969 Cup Final, Salford's last time at Wembley.

DO YOU KNOW?
What was the home town of Les Bettinson, former Salford player, coach and director? (Clue: it's the home of a famous old Amateur R.L. club.)

Five Star Favourites

GUS RISMAN
Star of the original "Red Devils" and one of the game's true legends.

LES BETTINSON
Played 319 games in 12 years for Salford and later served the club as coach.

DAVID WATKINS
One of the biggest ever recruits from Wales in 1967, went on to score 2907 points for the Reds in 407 games.

MAURICE RICHARDS
Welsh winger who played more games, and scored more tries, than any other man in Salford's history.

CHRIS HESKETH
12 years at the Willows from 1967 to 1979, he captained Salford and Great Britain and was a World Cup winner.

Club Nostalgia - SHEFFIELD

The Eagles first major trophy winning team- victorious in the Second Division Premiership Final at Old Trafford, a Sheffield side that lined up as: Gamson; Cartwright, Dickinson, Daryl Powell, Young; Aston, Close; Broadbent, Mick Cook, Gary Van Bellen, Sonny Nickle, Fleming and Smiles - with Steve Evans and Paul McDermott the substitutes.

Five Star Favourites

*MARK ASTON
"Mr. Sheffield Eagles," Mark was one of their early stars, a G.B. international, Lance Todd Trophy winner and driving force of the revived Eagles.

*DARYL POWELL
The club's most decorated player - original signing in 1984 who won 33 Test caps.

*SONNY NICKLE
The Eagles first big-money signing, he went on to win Great Britain honours.

*PAUL BROADBENT
Key man in the Wembley win of 1998 and another Eagles product to play for Great Britain.

*JOHNNY WOODCOCK
Excellent full-back and stalwart of the modern day Eagles.

(Above) After earlier disappointments, the Sheffield Eagles got a major sponsor on board in the late-1980s with backing from Whitbread breweries. This picture shows the initial cheque handover at the original home of Owlerton Stadium, by a Whitbread representative to Eagles founder Gary Hetherington and captain Daryl Powell.
(Right) STEVE LANE, contributed much to the Sheffield Eagles cause as a talented half-back in their early years.

DO YOU KNOW?

Who was coach of Sheffield Eagles when they won the Cup at Wembley in 1998?

Club Nostalgia - ST.HELENS

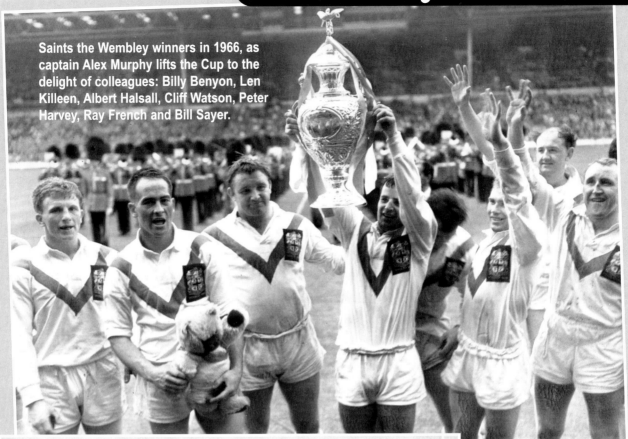

Saints the Wembley winners in 1966, as captain Alex Murphy lifts the Cup to the delight of colleagues: Billy Benyon, Len Killeen, Albert Halsall, Cliff Watson, Peter Harvey, Ray French and Bill Sayer.

(Above) St.Helens with the Lancashire Cup and Lancashire League trophies in the 1968-69 season. Left to right: *(Standing):* Billy Benyon, Cliff Watson, John Walsh, Graham Rees, Eric Chisnall, Bobby Wanbon, John Warlow, John Mantle, Frank Wilson, Jeff Hitchen, Cliff Evans (coach). *(Seated):* Cen Williams, Tony Barrow, Alan Whittle, Bill Sayer, Tommy Bishop, Austin Rhodes, Les Jones and Frank Myler.

(Right) GEORGE NICHOLLS and DEREK NOONAN in action for Saints in 1976.

DO YOU KNOW?

Who was the first St.Helens captain to lead them to a Challenge Cup Final victory? (Clue - it was in 1956.)

Five Star Favourites

*ALEX MURPHY
The one and only Alex - cocky, controversial, a teenage prodigy, he's one of the Saints true greats.

*TOM VAN VOLLENHOVEN
The flying Springbok scored 392 tries in 409 games for Saints.

*KEL COSLETT
Welsh full-back who made a record 519 appearances and set goal-kicking records, despite moving up into the pack.

*HARRY PINNER
Local boy who captained both St.Helens and Great Britain as superbly creative loose-forward.

* KIERON CUNNINGHAM
A star throughout the Super League era and pivotal to Saints' success.

Club Nostalgia - SWINTON

Swinton in 1982-83 as crowds began to look a bit sparse at the big Station Road ground. This Lions line-up includes such well known names as: Alan Fairhurst, Kevin O'Loughlin, Green Vigo, Les Bolton, Danny Wilson, Alva Drummond and Bob Irving, the ex-Oldham and Great Britain forward who was winding down his fine career.

Five Star Favourites

*ALBERT BLAN
Captain of the Lions in the two Championship seasons in the early 1960s. A fine leader, he played 16 years for Swinton.

*KEN GOWERS
Brilliant full-back who, in 18 seasons with Swinton, kicked a record 970 goals in a record 601 games.

*DAVE ROBINSON
Local Folly Lane junior was a great loose-forward, replacing Blan, and won 12 Great Britain Test caps.

*DANNY WILSON
The mercurial Welshman from Cardiff, starred in the 1980s - a maverick talent at stand-off.

*LES HOLLIDAY
Captained Swinton as they won a Premiership at Old Trafford in 1987, coached by his father Bill Holliday. Les also played for Gt.Britain.

(Left) Swinton made four Lancashire Cup Finals in five seasons in the early 'sixties, but each time met defeat by St.Helens.
(Right) Better luck at trophy-winning came in 1987 as winger DEREK BATE attacks in the Old Trafford Final.

(Left) KEN GOWERS

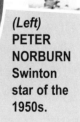

(Left) PETER NORBURN Swinton star of the 1950s.

DO YOU KNOW?
What was the native county of Swinton 1960s centre and later club chairman, Bob Fleet?

Club Nostalgia - WAKEFIELD TRINITY

Wakefield Trinity, on their way to Wembley in the spring of 1962, and not an empty space at Belle Vue. Left to right: *(Standing):* Gerry Round, Keith Holliday, Geoff Oakes, Brian Briggs, Dennis Williamson, Jack Wilkinson, Neil Fox. *(In front):* Alan Skene, Fred Smith, Harold Poynton, Derek Turner (captain), Albert Firth and Ken Hirst.

The spirit of youth in 1960 - Alan Skene, Keith Holliday and Harold Poynton snapped in Keswick on the way to a Cup quarter-final at Whitehaven.

DO YOU KNOW?
Which Wakefield Trinity coach got an Actors' union "Equity" card?

(Above) The mid-1970s at Belle Vue as MICK MORGAN leads the Trinity pack with ace stand-off DAVID TOPLISS looking on.

Five Star Favourites

*NEIL FOX
The game's leading points scorer. A dominant figure in Wakefield Trinity history

*DEREK TURNER
A key factor in the great Trinity era of the early 1960s. Wembley winning captain three times in four years.

*HAROLD POYNTON
"Fishcake" was the first man to lead Wakefield to a Championship title.

*DAVID TOPLISS
Very popular international stand-off, he guided Trinity to Wembley in 1979.

*WALLY LEWIS
He only played 10 games for the club, but the Aussie is still a legend in Wakefield.

Club Nostalgia - WARRINGTON

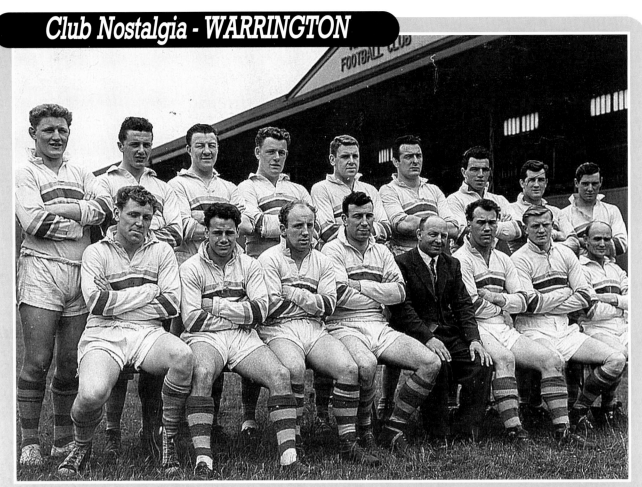

The Warrington team *circa* 1960 pictured at Wilderspool with their manager-coach Cec Mountford. Players in this team include: Alistair Brindle, Ally Naughton, Laurie Gilfedder and Harry Major; and on the front row: Martin Dickens, Bobby Greenhough, Jackie Edwards, Eric Fraser, Terry O'Grady, Jim Challinor and Brian Bevan.

Five Star Favourites

*BRIAN BEVAN
The greatest of all - scored an incredible 740 tries in 620 games for Warrington.

*ERIC FRASER
14 seasons at Wilderspool for this fine full-back, skippered Warrington and Great Britain.

*PARRY GORDON
One of the Wire's most loyal players, this big-hearted scrum-half played 19 seasons.

*JOHN BEVAN
The power-packed Welsh international winger was like Superman to Warrington fans in the 1970s and early '80s.

*PAUL CULLEN
Gave heart and soul to his hometown club for 16 seasons as a player, and later as coach.

DO YOU KNOW?

Who was Warrington's captain the last time they played in a Cup Final at Wembley?

(Above) Australian stars HARRY BATH and BRIAN BEVAN show the Challenge Cup to the Mayor of Warrington after the Wire's Wembley victory in 1950.
(Right) JONATHAN DAVIES on his way for a Warrington try in the mid-1990s with PAUL CULLEN in support - Wayne Kitchin is the chasing Workington Town defender.

Photo by EDDIE WHITHAM

Club Nostalgia - WHITEHAVEN

Whitehaven team from the mid-1980s pictured at the Recreation Ground. Left to right, *(Standing):* Milton Huddart, Billy Fisher, Stephen Burney, Bob Mackie, David Barnes, John Hartley, Joe Stewart. *(In front):* Steve Pythian, Frank Johnstone, Jimmy Dalton, Alan Banks, Colin Hall, Mel Mason, Tony D'Leny and Graham Cameron.

(Above) As the Whitehaven R.L. club celebrated its 60th birthday in August, 2008, it issued a reprint of its inaugral match programme from 1948.

DO YOU KNOW?

Who was the first overseas coach to be appointed by the Whitehaven club?

(Above) HARRY HUGHES playing for Whitehaven against his home town team Barrow in 1958. George Baker and Bill Smith are in support.

(Above, right) JOHN J. McKEOWN in action for Whitehaven. He scored a club record 2,133 points.

Five Star Favourites

*DICK HUDDART
One of the world's best forwards began his career at Whitehaven and remains the club's only Lions tourist.

*BILL HOLLIDAY
Another local forward who went on to captain Great Britain.

*ALEX CASSIE
Skilful little Scotsman who played 288 games for 'Haven.

*PHIL KITCHIN
Top class stand-off who played for Great Britain and captained 'Haven to a famous win over the Kiwi tourists in 1965.

* DAVID SEEDS
Modern day centre who set a new club career record of 225 tries in his 358 games for 'Haven.

Club Nostalgia - WIDNES

Widnes the Wembley winners in 1964 - among the players pictured are: Bobby Chisnall, Wally Hurstfield, Alan Briers, Vince Karalius, Frank Myler and George Kemel. The Chemics had just beaten Hull K.R. to win the Cup.

Five Star Favourites

*VINCE KARALIUS
After making his name with St.Helens, Vinty came home to Widnes and led them to Wembley victory in 1964.

*FRANK MYLER
Part of a Widnes footballing dynasty, he played 369 games in 12 years for the Chemics and famously represented Great Britain.

*DOUG LAUGHTON
Like Karalius and Myler, Douggie first captained and then coached Widnes, and led his national team.

*MICK ADAMS
A forward who had all the skills, he played 416 games in 13 years for Widnes and made Wmbley seem like a second home.

*MICK BURKE
Big attacking full-back who kicked 708 goals and scored 63 tries, winning every honour in his eight seasons with Widnes.

(Above) MICK BURKE playing at Wembley in 1984 with MICK ADAMS in support in what was his last ever game for Widnes before retiring.

(Right) PETER LYONS - one of the game's best known trainer-coaches, he was the Widnes mentor for over 20 years.

(Left) RAY DUTTON kicks at Wembley in 1975 - looking on is hooker Keith Elwell.

DO YOU KNOW?
Which Widnes player was in the "Guinness Book of Records" for making the most consecutive appearances.

Club Nostalgia - WIGAN

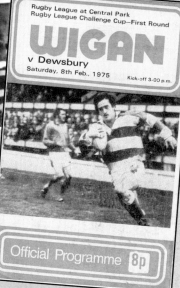

(Below) Wigan programme from February, 1975, with winger Jimmy Hornby pictured on the front cover.

(Above) Wigan team at Central Park in the 1957-58 season. Left to right, *(Standing):* Rees Thomas, Bernard McGurrin, Roy Evans, Brian McTigue, Alan Armstrong, Norman Cherrington, John Barton. *(Seated):* David Bolton, Terry O'Grady, Bill Sayer, Duncan Platt, Eric Ashton and Billy Boston.

DO YOU KNOW?

Who was Wigan's coach and assistant coach when they won the John Player trophy beating Leeds at Elland Road in 1983?

(Above) ERIC ASHTON interviewed by the BBC's David Coleman after the 1965 Wembley Cup Final.

(Left) The Iro brothers Kevin and Tony on the attack for Wigan in the 1989 Challenge Cup semi-final with Warrington at Maine Road. The Iros were just two of many players from New Zealand to make an impact on the Wigan club.

Five Star Favourites

*BILLY BOSTON
Billy remains an iconic figure in the history of Wigan. Scored 478 tries for the club over 14 wonderful years.

*ERIC ASHTON
The epitome of a "classic" centre, he led club and country with distinction, captaining Wigan in six Wembley Cup Finals.

*BRIAN McTIGUE
Wigan coal miner who was recognised as the best prop in the world after Lions tours in 1958 and 1962.

*ANDY GREGORY
Local St.Pats' boy who was scrum-half at the helm of the great Wigan late 1980s side.

*ELLERY HANLEY
Signed for Wigan in 1985 and built his reputation as the greatest modern era player.

Club Nostalgia - WORKINGTON

Workington Town in the mid-1970s. Left to right, *(Standing):* Harry Marland, John Risman, Ian Hartley, Ian Wright, Eddie Bowman, Les Gorley, Harold Henney, Bill McCracken. *(In front):* Arnold Walker, Iain MacCorquodale, Derek McMillan, Alan Banks, Paul Charlton (captain), Bobby Nicholson and Howard Allen. As a sign of changing times, no less than four of the above team won Great Britain Test caps and another two were Under-24 internationals. 14 of the 15 players pictured were local West Cumbrians, with Lancastrian MacCorquodale the only incomer.

Five Star Favourites

*IKE SOUTHWARD
Hailed from Ellenborough and gave a lifetime's service to Town. Twice a Lion and twice set a world transfer fee record

*BRIAN EDGAR
Three Lions tours and an Ashes series captain, one of the game's best forwards.

*BILL MARTIN
"Dickie" was a a crowd pleaser - big, tough prop, who played with a smile.

*PAUL CHARLTON
The game's finest running full-back, 18 Test caps and 727 games in a 20-year playing career - much of it with Workington Town.

*IAN WRIGHT
Probably the finest un-capped centre of his time, but did represent Great Britain Under-24s.

(Left) TONY PASKINS the Australian centre who was such a star in the Town glory days of the early 1950s.

(Right) Programme for Workington's 1951 Championship Final win at Maine Road.

(Below) Back in Manchester, coach Peter Walsh and captain "Buck" Armstrong enjoy Premiership victory at Old Trafford in 1994.

DO YOU KNOW?

Who was the South African winger who played for Town in the 1962 Western Final?

Club Nostalgia - YORK

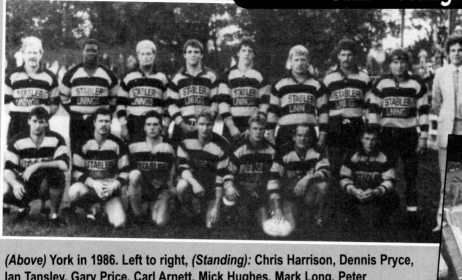

(Below) Programme for York's last game at the old Clarence Street ground in March, 1989.

(Above) York in 1986. Left to right, *(Standing):* Chris Harrison, Dennis Pryce, Ian Tansley, Gary Price, Carl Arnett, Mick Hughes, Mark Long, Peter Phillippo, Mr.John Stabler (director). *(In front):* ANO (unknown Aussie!), Wayne Morrell, Brian Walters, Andy Mercer, Paul Prendiville and Ian Wilson.

(Left) WILLIE HARGREAVES, the full-back who was such a pivotal figure in York teams for over 13 years. Willie hailed from Wakefield, but played more games than anybody else in York's history, with 448 matches between 1952-53 and 1965-66.

(Below) BASIL WATTS in action in one of his 354 games for York - he was one of Great Britain's first World Cup winning heroes of 1954.

Five Star Favourites

*BASIL WATTS
York lad who became a World Cup hero in France in 1954. One of the best forwards at Clarence St.

*VIC YORKE
Aptly named prop with a mighty boot which kicked a record 1,060 goals in 13 seasons with York.

*JEFF STEVENSON
Was a York player when he captained Britain to the Ashes for the last time in 1959.

* GEOFF SMITH
Prolific try-scoring winger who represented Yorkshire and Great Britain in the 1963 Ashes

*GRAHAM STEADMAN
Points scoring stand-off star of the mid 1980s, helped York to go close to Wembley in '84.

DO YOU KNOW?

What was the York club renamed when they first left Clarence Street to move to the new stadium in 1989?

(Above) PAUL McDERMOTT as a York player in September, 1981. Paul also turned out for Sheffield, Whitehaven and Rochdale and his brother Brian played for Bradford and Great Britain.

WOULD YOU BELIEVE IT?

STRANGE BUT TRUE - FUNNY TALES FROM THE HISTORY OF RUGBY LEAGUE

It wasn't exactly the example to set before his pupils when schoolmaster Jack Kitching was sent-off for punching an opponent in the first post-War Test match at the Sydney Cricket Ground in 1946. Kitching, had a reputation as a gentleman, who later became a Grammar School headmaster and ran for Parliament as a Liberal candidate. Playing in the centre for Bradford Northern he was usually well away from any skullduggery that went on among the forwards, but Jack flipped that day in Sydney when he was bitten by an opposing player. There's no truth in the rumour that, after his long walk to the dressing-room in Sydney, teacher Jack made himself go to the blackboard and write a hundred lines: *"I must not punch in retaliation when some Aussie b****** bites me!"*

Jack Kitching on his long walk off in Sydney on the 1946 tour.

* * * * * *

WHEN Eddie Waring took on the job as secretary-manager of Dewsbury, his first job was to scrounge £136 to pay players' wages from the previous season. During the war years when Eddie put together a star-studded Dewsbury team full of well known guest players, with money very tight some of them got paid in meat - rationing was very strict but Eddie had good contacts with the local butchers! Imagine the pre-match dressing-room conversation at Crown Flatt - *"Right lads, today's winning bonus is going to be two lamb chops and half a pound of liver!"*

* * * * * *

TALKING of incentives ... the Huddersfield committee got quite a surprise when they were in deep discussions with Swinton's all-time great forward Martin Hodgson about a move to Fartown in the twilight of his career. A huge figure, big Martin had terrorised the Australian pack as Britain won the Ashes throughout the 1930s, and some of the Huddersfield gentlemen were a bit wary of upsetting him if their offer did not match his expectations. But, when they got down to the nitty-gritty and asked what kind of "sweetener" he would require to make the transfer go through, they were shocked when all he asked for was a double-pram. Having become the father of young twins that's what he said he needed ... and that's what he got!

IMAGINE this headline in 2008 - *"Hunslet hoping to sign Newcastle United star."* What? Michael Owen heading for the South Leeds Stadium? In the multi-million pound world of football now, it just couldn't happen, and - sadly - Hunslet are no longer the power they were in the world of Rugby League. But back in the early 1950s, Hunslet - full of self confidence - genuinely did make an offer to Geordie football legend Jackie Milburn to switch to Rugby League and come and join them at Parkside. Milburn was one of the biggest names in English football but was in dispute with the Newcastle club at the time and was left twiddling his thumbs on Saturday afternoons. Apparently the terms offered by Hunslet were good enough, but Jackie didn't fancy Rugby League saying it was *"a bit too rough."*

Jackie Milburn - Geordie star was a Hunslet target.

* * * * * *

KEIGHLEY forward Geoff Crewdson was a big lad in his playing days, and when he was selected to go on tour with the Great Britain team in 1966 he had to have his shirt specially made to fit his 17-stone frame. Another big prop, Bill Martin from Workington, did not enjoy the same luxury when he made his one and only Test match appearance for Great Britain in France in 1962. Bill's off-the-peg shirt was so tight he could hardly move his arms, which was a clear disadvantage for him on the day in a match that turned into a Perpignan bloodbath with big French forwards like Aldo Quaglio and Jean Barthe running amock!

* * * * * *

TALKING of big lads, the famous "Indomitables" tour to Australia in 1946 caused a stir when they finally arrived in Sydney after their long journey. With Britain still in the grip of post-War rationing, the Australians had been very generous in sending food parcels across to the "mother country" to help their starving cousins and, as they awaited the arrival of the British tourng team, Aussie League officials had visions of a bunch of skinny, mal-nourished young Pommies stepping off the train from Perth. Imagine their shock when the first to alight at Sydney station was the big prop Ken Gee, followed by the huge figure of Bradford's Frank Whitcombe. The Aussie jaws dropped and a voice among them was heard to say: *"Right, that's it, no more bloody food parcels to England - there's obviously no food shortage over there anymore!"*

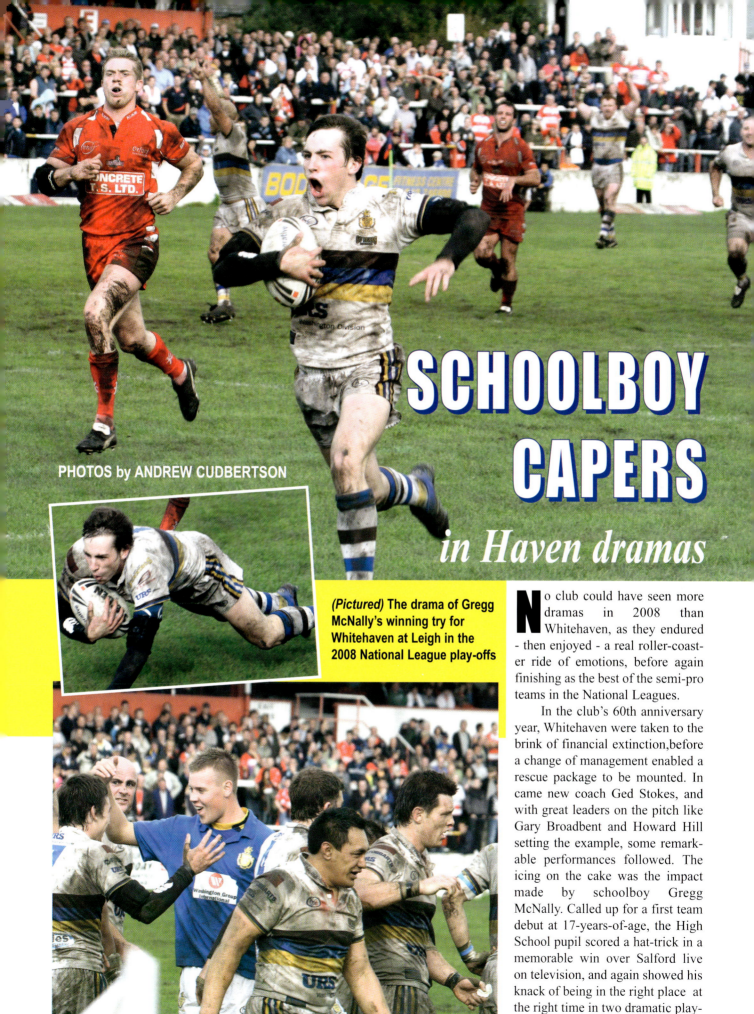

SCHOOLBOY CAPERS
in Haven dramas

PHOTOS by ANDREW CUDBERTSON

(Pictured) The drama of Gregg McNally's winning try for Whitehaven at Leigh in the 2008 National League play-offs

No club could have seen more dramas in 2008 than Whitehaven, as they endured - then enjoyed - a real roller-coaster ride of emotions, before again finishing as the best of the semi-pro teams in the National Leagues.

In the club's 60th anniversary year, Whitehaven were taken to the brink of financial extinction, before a change of management enabled a rescue package to be mounted. In came new coach Ged Stokes, and with great leaders on the pitch like Gary Broadbent and Howard Hill setting the example, some remarkable performances followed. The icing on the cake was the impact made by schoolboy Gregg McNally. Called up for a first team debut at 17-years-of-age, the High School pupil scored a hat-trick in a memorable win over Salford live on television, and again showed his knack of being in the right place at the right time in two dramatic play-off wins at Leigh and Halifax.

After Wigan glory years
JASON LED THE EXODUS

Jason Robinson in action for England at Wembley in the 1995 Rugby League World Cup.

WHEN WIGAN WERE THE WORLD CLUB CHAMPIONS

It was a night Wigan will never forget, and nobody more than their sparkling little winger Jason Robinson. The night Wigan's record-breaking era of success - which had lasted for the best part of a decade - came to its most glorious climax on 1st June, 1994 when they were crowned World Club Champions by beating the Brisbane Broncos on their own Queensland turf. And the night when Jason Robinson's reputation as a world star was cemented - true, Jason had already made a two-try Test debut for Great Britain against New Zealand at Wembley in the autumn of 1993, but in the world of Rugby League it's the hardbitten

Australians who set the standards. The Aussies knew little about "Billy Whizz" as Wigan walked out to take on their club champions in Brisbane, but by the end of the match they had no doubts about one of the most sparkling attacking players the game had produced.

Jason scored just the one try in Wigan's 20-14 victory over the Broncos - and on the facing page that magical moment is captured by the camera as he touches down to the delight of his team-mate, hooker Martin Hall. But, much more than that, Robinson's elusiveness, trickery, and sheer "jack in a box" power, packed into such a compact frame, had made the watching Australians sit up and take note. It was as much in surprise as admiration, because Aussie self-confidence had grown to the point where they could hardly believe any Englishman could be better than their own players and the Aussies just didn't have anybody who could do what Jason Robinson did.

Wigan's tremendous run of success in the years leading up to 1994 had done so much to promote a positive new image for Rugby League in Britain, and their victory in the World Club Championship in Brisbane put the seal on a build up that had effectively begun when they won the Challenge Cup at Wembley in 1985 for the first time in twenty years. These were the days before Super League and, significantly, of the 17 Wigan players who won that world title 14 were English players (many of them local lads) with just the three New Zealanders: Botica, Panapa and Tuigamala, adding an overseas flavour.

For the record, the Wigan team who stunned Brisbane and a crowd of 54,220 people that night in 1994 was:
Gary Connolly; Jason Robinson, Sam Panapa, Barrie-Jon Mather, Martin Offiah; Frano Botica, Shaun Edwards (captain); Neil Cowie, Martin Dermott, Billy McGinty, Denis Betts, Andrew Farrell and Phil Clarke.
Substitutes: **Va'aiga Tuigamala, Martin Hall, Paul Atcheson and Mick Cassidy.**

Take a look at the sheer joy on the faces of those Wigan players pictured on the facing page - they were kings of the Rugby League world. Fast forward now to the year 2008 and who could have predicted that so many of those players would have crossed over to Rugby Union? As either players or coaches, no less than eleven of them found their way into the 15-aside game at the top level - three of those (Robinson, Mather and Farrell) became England internationals in Rugby Union whilst Shaun Edwards is now regarded as one of the world's leading coaches in Rugby Union.

In 1994 it would have been impossible to believe that Jason Robinson, the darting little winger who started out playing junior Rugby League in Hunslet, would one day be regarded as the darling of the Twickenham hordes after

(Above) Denis Betts on the ball for Wigan in their famous victory over the Brisbane Broncos in 1994. Denis is one of the most recent converts to Rugby Union where he can now be found in a coaching capacity with the Gloucester club. Strangely, the BBC no longer appear to regard him as a perfect voice for broadcasting when it comes to his new game.

becoming the captain of England's "rugger" team. Well, almost as hard to believe as the thought that Central Park would disappear to become a Tesco's or that Wigan Rugby League club would be forced out of their own home ground for an important play-off match under orders from Wigan Athletic. But that is what happened to Jason - after everything started to change in the world of both codes of rugby after the dramas of 1995.

Whilst other players made the switch to Rugby Union before him, it truly was Jason Robinson who led the exodus in terms of the sheer impact he made on the Union game - and so quickly. After just a handful of club games for Sale he was in the England team, and after just 72 minutes on the field for England, he was selected for the 2001 British Lions touring team to Australia. His debut match for the Lions produced a remarkable record five tries, and in his Test debut, it took him just three minutes to leave his opposite winger for dead and score a try that left Rugby Union correspondents gasping for superlatives.

Two years later, Robinson was back in Australia and played an absolutely key role in England winning the Rugby Union World Cup (so key, in fact, that he appeared to be England's only player capable of scoring a try or beating a defender to make a break.) His status as national hero was confirmed, and Jason has been a wonderful ambassador for his new game, and his country.

Looking back to 1994, Wigan's triumph in becoming World Champions can be regarded even more as a pinnacle for British club Rugby League - but what League fans can't quite understand is just why a team who peaked fully 14 years ago should still be proving such a source of fascination and personnel for Rugby Union.

SEE RUGBY LEAGUE HISTORY

Come alive on DVD

YOUR CHANCE TO SEE AGAIN SOME HISTORIC RUGBY LEAGUE EVENTS

A large selection of DVDs now available which bring to life some of the great moments in Rugby League history. Including famous Test matches, Ashes battles and Wembley Cup Finals, plus historical documentaries.

Challenge Cup Finals include: 1962, 1963, 1965, 1967, 1968, 1969, 1970, 1971, 1972, 1973, 1978, 1979, 1982, 1985, 1986 and 1987 -
All available on DVD price £17.95 (plus £1.50 p&p).
(Titles also available on Video)
See our website - or to receive a free illustrated catalogue listing all titles available, send a first class stamp to:

Open Rugby Nostagia, P.O.Box 22, Egremont, Cumbria, CA23 3WA
Or contact us by e-mail at: openrugby.nostalgia@virgin.net

To view more details - or order on-line via secure payment - see our website:
www.openrugbynostalgia.com

Step into the Rugby League

TIME TUNNEL

Memories of Rugby League in years gone by

Action from England versus France at Fartown, Huddersfield, October, 1947.

KEEPING THE CLARET AND GOLD IN THE SPOTLIGHT

THE HUDDERSFIELD TRADITION

Different generations have come and gone, but one thing has always remained rock solid in the Yorkshire town of Huddersfield - the spirit of the *Claret and Gold.* In this, the birthplace of Rugby League, the traditions of the Huddersfield club maintain a position akin to royalty in the eyes of those who have studied the game's history.

Young players at Fartown always knew they were following in some mighty famous footsteps, and carried on their shoulders the responsibility of maintaining the honour of the claret and gold first established by the successfu teams and wonderful players of the past. The ghosts of Wagstaff, Douglas Clark, Ben Gronow and company were never far away, just as more recent generations would have to live up to the deeds of the Pat Devery, Lionel Cooper, Dave Valentine era. That meant there was always something special about being a Huddersfield player and wearing the claret and gold. Look at the optimism in the faces of the lads *(pictured above)* stepping out at Fartown for their first training run ahead of a new season. Hope always sprang eternal, and this photograph was taken in the summer of 1968. A young Billy Pickup leads the group and the other players behind him are, *from left to right:* Graham Naylor, Billy Gill, Graham Starkey, Don Close, Richard Wallace, Malcolm Breakespeare, Bob

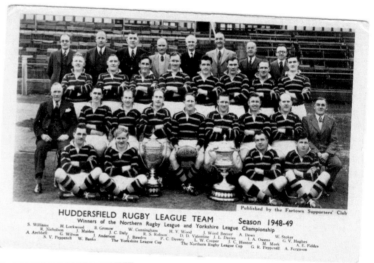

Taylor. Arnie Long, Bruce Leek and Ken Senior. The last named has, subsequently, done as much as anybody to maintain those Fartown traditions as a leading figure in the Huddersfield Players' Association. Huddersfield always were in the spotlight - at the top of this page you can see their skipper Pat Devery featured on the front cover of the *"Rugby League Gazette"* in 1951. Whilst *(above)* a postcard issued by the Fartown Supporters' Club bearing a specially posed team photo of the 1948-49 Championship winners and *(left)* Russ Pepperell proudly holding the Challenge Cup after victory at Wembley in 1953.

IKE'S WEMBLEY CAPTURED ON FILM

It was one of Wembley's most dramatic images - in the 1958 Cup Final - as Workington winger Ike Southward stretched high to take a pass, his team-mate Harry Archer had just been laid out by Wigan's Mick Sullivan. As we can see from the wider panoramic picture *(above)* the touch-judge could hardly have had a closer view, but he saw nothing and the flag stayed down. Meanwhile, the photographer marked with an asterik* was perfectly placed to capture the famous photograph *(right)* of Ike's athleticism in all its glory.

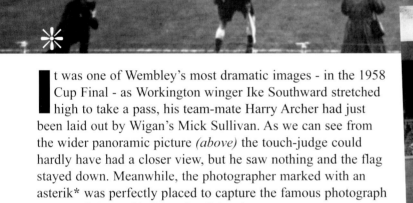

Martin Offiah scored more tries than any other Englishman in the history of Rugby League - but none was better than this one *(pictured, left)* which put the seal on the Championship for Widnes in 1989. The Chemics had to beat Wigan at Naughton Park to clinch the title, and they did it in style with a magnificent run by Offiah leading to this triumphant dive over in the corner at the Lowerhouse Lane end of the ground. Widnes went on to become World Club Champions that year.

OFFIAH FLIES

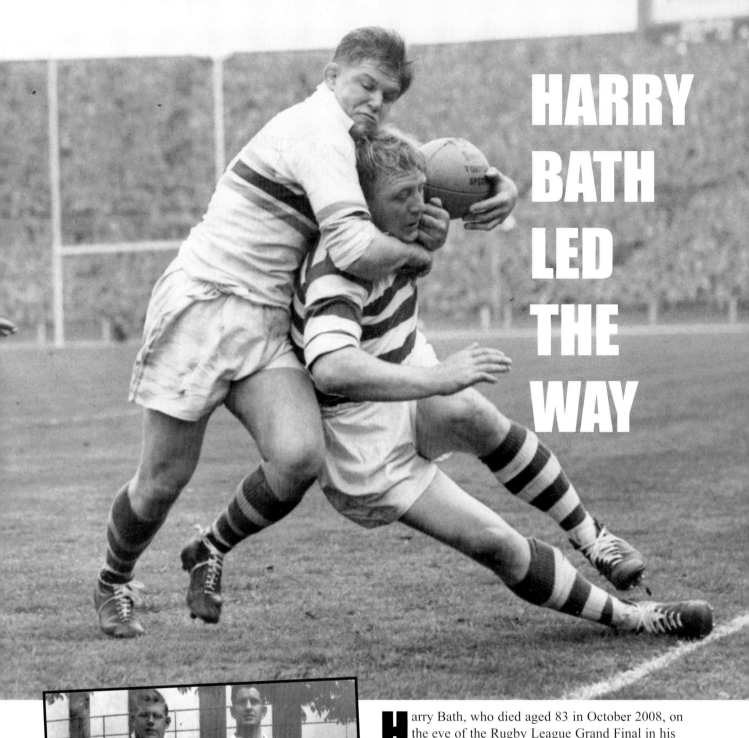

HARRY BATH LED THE WAY

(Above) A rare private photo of Harry Bath with fellow Australian second-row partner Johnny Mudge, in France whilst on duty for a British Empire X111. This picture was taken on his own camera by their team-mate Tony Paskins.

Harry Bath, who died aged 83 in October 2008, on the eve of the Rugby League Grand Final in his native Australia, will always be remembered as one of the great pioneers of the world game. Harry became the first Australian to captain a team to Challenge Cup victory at Wembley when he led Warrington against Widnes in 1950, and he was also one of the major figures in the famous Other Nationalities team which contributed so much to the European International Championship. When he returned home to Australia in 1957 he set about shaping the great St.George team and later was a very successful coach - including guiding Australia to the World Cup in 1968. The picture (above) shows Harry Bath bringing down a Halifax forward in the 1954 Wembley Final - nobody worried about the "grapple tackle" in those days! After this Final was drawn 4-all, the two teams met agan in the famous replay at Odsal Stadium which drew a record crowd of over 102,000.

DERBY DAYS IN THE CITY OF KINGSTON-UPON-HULL

(Above) The biggest derby match of them all, when Hull and Hull Kingston Rovers met at Wembley in he 1980 Challenge Cup Final. The picture shows referee Fred Lindop indicating "no try" even though Hull's hooker Ron Wileman had got over the Rovers line. Alan Agar and Roy Holdstock had made the tackle with winger Steve Hubbard lending a helping hand. The others Robins in the picture are Paul Rose, David Watkinson and Phil Lowe, with Hull F.C.'s Charlie Stone and Keith Tindall appealing to Mr. Lindop to see things differently. For those who don't know, Rovers won 10-5 that day!

HULL RIVALS

In the present day game there's absolutely no doubt that one of the best things to happen to the Super League was getting Hull K.R. into it. Rovers' presence has played a big part in boosting attendance averages, as they guarantee their cross-city rivals Hull F.C. a full house of 23,000-plus everytime they stage a derby at the K.C.Stadium. Added to that, the Robins take a large away support to every ground they visit. Such is the passion for Rugby League in the city of Hull, and derby days are stll something very special. In years gone by, derbies at the Boulevard on Christmas Day or at Craven Park on Good Friday, were very different for the players - many of whom were local Hull lads who worked together and, often, socialised together. These two pictures on the right will stir a few memories for fans of both Hull and Hull Kingston Rovers.

(Above) Four young players arrive at the Boulevard in 1950, Cox, Whiteley, Mick Scott and Clark. Who would have known then that Johnny Whiteley would go on to become such a legend in the city of Hull? *(Below)* The Hull K.R. team in the 1960-61 season, skippered by Harry Poole, the player on his right is scrum-half Arthur Bunting, later to be the coach of the black and whites in their glory years of the 1980s.

WHEN WORKINGTON & WHITEHAVEN COMBINED TO TACKLE THE AUSSIES

CUMBRIANS UNITED

(Above) Action from a Cumberland derby between Workington Town (in the dark jerseys) and Whitehaven at Derwent Park in 1958 - just a year before the two local rival clubs combined to play the Australian touring team on the same pitch.

Players from Workington and Whitehaven were always used to getting together to play for the Cumberland County team, when invariably they would be joined by some illustrious names from Lancashire or Yorkshire clubs who rallied to the call of their native county. Initially, those names would include some of the Huddersfield aces Jeff Bawden, Bob Nicholson and Russ Pepperell; later it might be Alvin Ackerley and Geoff Palmer from Halifax or the fearsome Drake brothers and Ivor Watts from Hull; then the ever loyal Don Wilson from Barrow and superstar Dick Huddart from St.Helens.

But it was a "first" when Workington and Whitehaven players alone were asked to combine to make up a team to play the 1959 Australian touring team. The fixture was at Workington's Derwent Park - the first time Town's new ground had the chance to host a touring team and the previous Kangaroo tourists in 1956 had played just Whitehaven (who beat the Aussies 14-11) on their only visit to Cumberland. So it was not "Cumberland" or even a "Cumbrian X111" who tackled the Australians in 1959, but a "Workington and Whitehaven" combined selection. The Aussies were coming straight off the back of their impressive First Test victory over Great Britain at Swinton the previous Saturday, and were skippered for the first time by Brian Hambly, who scored the crucial try in the second-half which paved the way for a 13-8 victory. The game was played on a Thursday afternoon, with a 3pm kick-off, and the attendance was 7,463. The local selection wore Workington Town's kit of white jerseys with a blue band, and their eight points came from tries by Hughes and Gibson and just one goal from Lowden.

AFTER two of Town's 1958 Lions tourists - Bill Wookey and Brian Edgar - were late injury withdrawals, the make-up of the combined side was six players from the host club Workington and seven from Whitehaven. The team was: Syd Lowden (Workington.); Harry Hughes (W'haven), John O'Neil (Workington.), Eppie Gibson (W'haven) captain, Ron Stephenson (W'haven); Harry Archer (Workington), Sol Roper (Workington); Bill McAlone (W'haven), Jim Lynch (W'haven), Bill Martin (Workington), Cec Thompson (Workington) John Tembey (W'haven), Bill Holliday (W'haven).

SNOW PATROL

Welcome to Ice-Station Odsal. This winter's day in Bradford was in the early 1950s, as Northern entertained Castleford, with loose-forward Ken Traill getting the ball kicked downfield. In the background, only a handful of spectators had braved the open terrace as the prospect of a blizzard loomed.

In the days when winters were a lot colder, having to play in snow was an occasional occupational hazard for Rugby League players. The grounds furthest above sea level, notably Thrum Hall, Odsal and the Watersheddings, were usually the worst hit. It didn't happen very often, but when the snow did come it made for spectacular pictures.

(Right) Wigan's Bill Francis on the attack against Leeds at a snow covered Headingley in the 1976-77 season. The Wigan man in support is prop Brian Hogan, whilst Stan Fearnley is the Leeds loose-forward covering across. Thanks to its undersoil heating in the 1960s and '70s, Headingley was often the only ground playable if a cold snap of heavy frost set in.

(Left) There's just a dusting of snow on the Recreation Ground pitch in this picture from the 1957 Challenge Cup tie between Whitehaven and Hunslet. Arthur Clues is the man bringing down Whitehaven's Geoff Robinson just short of the line in a match that has become known as the "Ice Bowl game." It was so cold, players had to be revived with brandy at half-time, and Hunslet forward Brian Shaw collapsed with hypothermia.

CLASSY CAS'

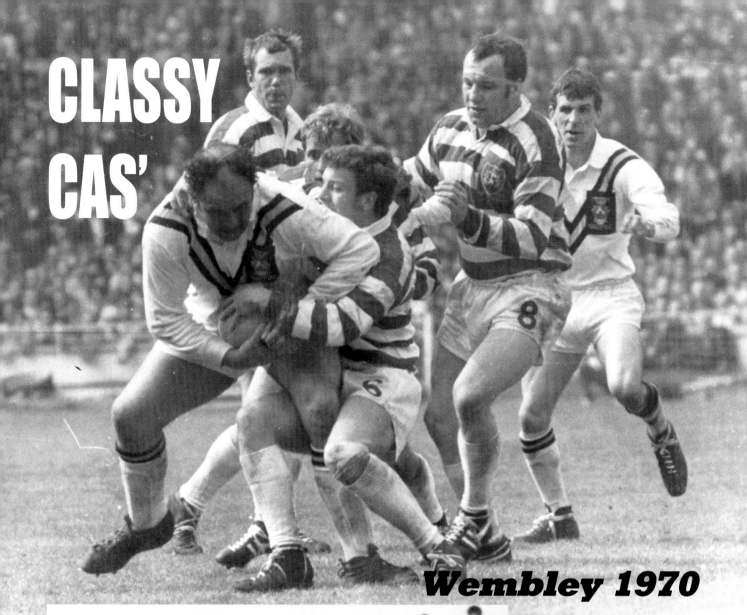

Wembley 1970

and Heppy stars for Great Britain

(Above) KEITH HEPWORTH pictured on the attack for Great Britain against Australia in the 1970 World Cup Final at Headingley. "Heppy" had played a key role in the outstanding British team winning the Ashes on tour earlier that year, but they could not repeat that form in this World Cup Final and went down to the Aussies in a bruiser.

It was a very good year for Castleford players in 1970. First of all, they went back to Wembley and retained the Cup they had won against Salford the previous year. Pictured *(above)* Cas' prop Dennis Hartley in the 1970 Final proving a handful for the Wigan defenders - half-backs Frankie Parr and David Hill, with forwards Keith Ashcroft and Dave Robinson looking on next to Castleford skipper Alan Hardisty. Big Dennis then was one of several Cas' players, most notably Malcolm Reilly and Keith Hepworth, who played important parts in Great Britain winning the Ashes in Australia. Alongside them was one of Castleford's greatest products - Roger Millward (then a Hull K.R. player.)

WAKEFIELD - THE MERRIE CITY OF THE 'SIXTIES

TRINITY TALES

No team in Rugby League was more symbolic of the change from the 1950s to the 'sixties than Wakefield Trinity. It must have been fun to be a young person growing up in the Merrie City at the time when Belle Vue was being packed on Saturday afternoons to see the exploits of "Rocky" Turner and his great team, and then enjoy three adventures to London in four years to see Neil Fox, Alan Skene and company win the Challenge Cup. Time moved on and "Rocky" retired, to be replaced as captain by Harold Poynton, who led another fine Trinity side to their first ever Championships and a return to Wermbley for the heartbreak of the "Watersplash" Final in 1968. The picture at the top of the page is from that 1968 Cup run, the quarter-final against Castleford at Belle Vue, with Poynton in possession supported by South African favourite Gert "Oupa" Coetzer.

Trinity's captain Derek Turner is presented with the Yorkshire Cup in 1960 - to give him the full set of all six winners medals.

Wakefield at Wembley in 1960 as winger John Etty is presented to the Duke of Edinburgh.

LANCASHIRE GIANTS

ST.HELENS v WIGAN

Good Friday, 1960, and St.Helens play Wigan at Knowsley Road in one of the most eagerly awaited fixtures of every season. The Saints back-line are looking dangerous *(above)* as centre John Donovan draws the defence and puts his fellow centre Ken Large (number three) away. Ominously for Wigan, Tom Van Vollenhoven looms unmarked on the outside as his fellow South African, Fred Griffiths - the Wigan full-back - frantically tries to cover across, as does big prop John Barton. It's one of those moments when you can see the drama unfolding before your very eyes, and a 30,000 crowd were jammed into Knowsley Road to enjoy it.

WARRINGTON v SWINTON

Photo by EDDIE WHITHAM

(Above) Warrington winger Brian Glover tackles his opposite number from Swinton, John Speed, as the Wire met the Lions at Wilderspool in the mid-1960s. This was a time when Swinton were still one of the top sides in Lancashire.

FOR FANS WHO DON'T WANT TO FORGET
GREAT STORIES, GREAT OLD PICTURES & GREAT MEMORIES

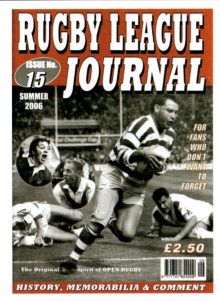
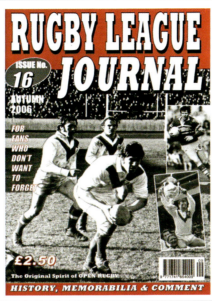
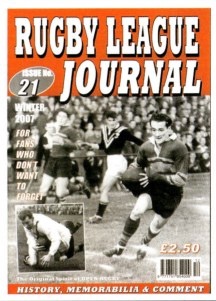

CATCH UP ON YOUR READING - BACK ISSUES AVAILABLE

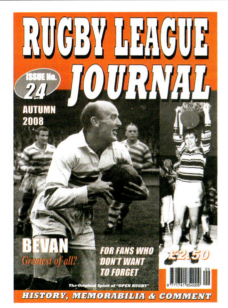
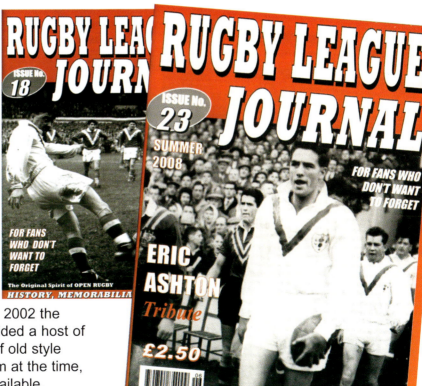

In the six years since its launch in 2002 the *"Rugby League Journal"* has provided a host of excellent reading and memories of old style Rugby League. If you missed them at the time, numerous Back-Issues are still available. Don't miss these superb collectors' items.

ALL BACK-ISSUES PRICE £3.50 EACH *(incl. p&p.)*

Numerous different Back Issues are still available, including all the issues pictured on this page. To order Back issues at £3.50 each, send cheque/P.O. *(payable to 'Rugby League Journal')* to: Rugby League Journal, P.O.Box 22, Egremont, Cumbria, CA23 3WA
E-mail: rugbyleague.journal@virgin.net   See our website at: www.rugbyleaguejournal.net

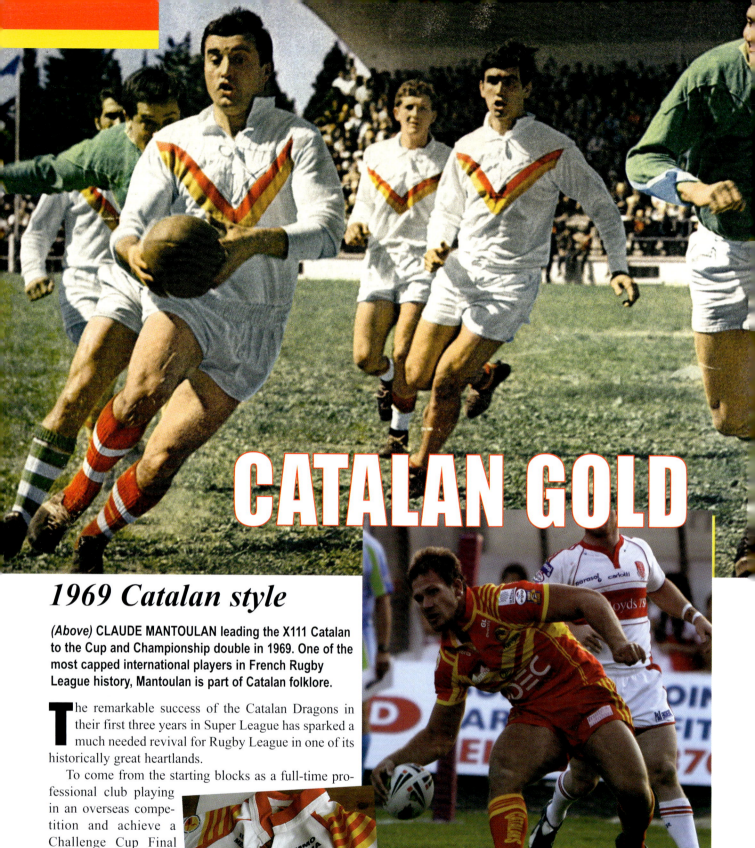

CATALAN GOLD

1969 Catalan style

(Above) CLAUDE MANTOULAN leading the X111 Catalan to the Cup and Championship double in 1969. One of the most capped international players in French Rugby League history, Mantoulan is part of Catalan folklore.

The remarkable success of the Catalan Dragons in their first three years in Super League has sparked a much needed revival for Rugby League in one of its historically great heartlands.

To come from the starting blocks as a full-time professional club playing in an overseas competition and achieve a Challenge Cup Final place in their second season and a top-three finish in the Super League in their third, is a great credit to the Catalans club, and way ahead of even their most optimistic predictions. In the process, the Catalan Dragons project

PHOTO by ANDREW VARLEY PICTURE AGENCY

2008 Catalan style

(Above) The Dragons jersey in 2008, still carrying the proud "blood and gold" colours of the Catalans. *(Above, right)* GREGORY MOUNIS touches down for a try for the Catalan Dragons in 2008 against Hull K.R. Mounis is a local Perpignan junior now an established professional.

has been very successful in achieving the primary aim behind its creation - that of rebuilding a presence for the Rugby League code in France as a serious professional sport. That presence, of course, is currently limited to the surrounds of the city of Perpignan, although the Catalan Dragons also draw their support from groups of diehard Rugby League fans from other towns in the south of France who now think they are in dreamland at being able to watch in the flesh the very best that the Super League has to offer.

Tied in with that aim is the belief that having a successful Super League club in France will have a direct influence on improving the French national team - enabling a group of French players to be full-time professionals playing in a high-pressure competition every week is sure to equip them better to make France competitive again when they play the leading nations of Australia, New Zealand and England. The short term problem - as was emphasised by France's heavy defeat at home to England during the summer of 2008 - is that the Catalan Dragons cannot supply all seventeen regular first-team players to the French national team, and so France desperately needs to be allowed to build a second Super League franchise (as was vainly hoped for at Toulouse) to be able to develop more full-time professional players.

All this has become necessary, of course, because the French domestic Rugby League competition can no longer do this as it has dwindled to just a pale shadow of what it used to be, with many less active clubs, many less players, far smaller support and hardly any media coverage outside its most local levels.

The way the Catalan Dragons have managed to buck that trend and turn Rugby League's downward spiral around so spectacularly in the Perpignan area has been a stunning success story - a lesson for British Rugby League officials in the merits of strategically building Super League franchises in places which have long been heartlands of the game, with a very personal emotional attachment to its history and a considerable latent support and pool of junior playing talent just waiting to be tapped into. (Does the word "Cumbria" ring any bells here?)

In the space of three years, the Catalans have gone from a zero starting point to a situation where they have attracted capacity 9,000 crowds to their Gilbert Brutus stadium which is now scheduled for further development so its capacity can be increased. Of even greater significance to those in France where rugby clubs are always heavily dependent on financial support from their local councils and local government bodies, is the way Perpignan has now recognised the Catalan Dragons in the same breath as U.S.A.P. (their Rugby Union team.)

The Dragons players, especially their imports from Australia and New Zealand, have noticed things change in that recognition over the past three years. When they arrived, U.S.A.P. ruled the roost in Perpignan, but now the Rugby League team are up there with them in terms of public and local media respect and enthusiasm.

That is a heart-warming revival because, for so many years, Rugby League used to be top-dog in Perpignan. Catalans were instrumental in the very birth of the 13-aside game in France and Perpignan's own club, *XIII Catalan*, born on 24th August, 1934, were founder members of the French Rugby League and always at the forefront of the game.

(Above) BERNARD GUASCH as a player for X111 Catalan 30 years ago in 1978 - now the President of the Catalan Dragons.

Whilst 2008 saw the Catalan Dragons fill their Gilbert Brutus stadium to its current capacity of just over 9,000, the record attendance for a rugby match of either code in the city of Perpignan remains the near 20,000 who packed the Brutus in 1967 for the Lord Derby Cup Final between *XIII Catalan* and Carcassonne. An official figure of 16,250 paying spectators was recorded that day in a match refereed by the Englishman Eric Clay.

In some ways it is ironic that the Catalans are now the key driving force in trying to rebuild Rugby League's status in France, because it was the Catalans of an earlier vintage who did much to damage it - it was *XIII Catalan* who took most of the blame for events leading up to the infamous Championship Final of 1981 which was abandoned after just four minutes due to a wild brawl. The hot-tempered Catalans brought the game to its knees back then and precipitated the wider media and television's excuse for ignoring Rugby League in France which was to have such a weakening long-term effect.

For *XIII Catalan* things eventually got so bad that - faced with enormous financial problems - they were forced in 1998 to merge with their neighbours from St.Esteve, and the new entity called *Union Treiziste Catalane* was formed. With their crowds having slipped to below the 1,000 mark whilst U.S.A.P. had grown to have around 10,000 season ticket holders and enormous income from sponsorship, Rugby League in Perpignan was on the ropes as a pathetic shadow of its former strength.

Now, in the space of three years of the Catalan Dragons, all that has changed and the 13-aside game in Perpignan can hold its head very high. The Catalans have always been known by their famous triblal colours of the *sang et or*, which translated means "blood and gold." Plenty of blood may have been spilt over the past 74 years in the cause of Catalan Rugby League, but in 2008 it seems to have really struck gold.

Amateur Rugby League in 2008

Amateur Rugby League participants had much to aim for on the international front in 2008 but, sadly - in a year when the 25th anniversary was celebrated of one of the most famous of all BARLA tours - many young players found the experience of representing their country overseas rather less fulfilling. Whilst back in 1983 the BARLA Young Lions led by Garry Schofield, Deryck Fox, Michael Ford, Gary Divorty and company were famously playing the full might of the Junior Kiwis in Tests at Carlaw Park, their 2008 equivalents (the BARLA Under-18s) found themselves retsricted to an Australian tour itinerary of games against members of the Penrith District Junior League.

Earlier, BARLA had again supported development efforts in Italy by sending a squad of Under-23s to take part in an international tournament, only to find the standard of organisation and opposing teams fell way short of the levels these talented and dedicated young British players deserve when they reach the pinnacle of being picked for their country.

The BARLA Open-Age player-of-the-year was Trevor Penrose, a prop-forward from Skirlaugh (who followed in some very illustrious footsteps in winning this award) whilst the Youth player-of-the-year was Dave Manning from Dewsbury Celtic.

Political battles have ensured BARLA has been undermined since those heady days of the 1983 Young Lions and their various pioneering tours to Papua New Guinea, and in 2008 more international fixtures were offered to the "Great Britain Community Lions" teams - organised and financed under the auspices of the Rugby Football League's community board, but still almost totally dependent on players from BARLA clubs.

At Open-Age level, the "Community Lions" lost at home to France at Widnes, after achieving a noteworthy victory over the French at Beziers earlier in the season. They then set out during the summer for a trip to Australia to take part in a tournament called the "Quad Series," against three Aussie selections: NSW Country; Queensland Country and the *Jim Beam Cup* representative side. Unfortunately, the British Amateurs were well beaten in their games against all three. This Great Britain side was captained and coached by the Wigan duo of Mel Alker and Jimmy Taylor. Meanwhile at youth level (under-18s) the Great Britain "Community Lions" also lost at home to the French Juniors (at Whitehaven) after coming back with a very creditable draw against the same opposition in Pamiers earlier in the season.

Domestically, Cumbria won the Amateur County Championship, ending Yorkshire's three-year reign as Champions. In fact, Cumbria won the titles at both Open-Age and Youth levels. The Cumbrians went on to enjoy their own summer tour of Australia.

East Hull were the undoubted top Amateur club in 2008 - winning a tremendous Cup and League double. The Hull side, coached by well known Super League players Lee Radford and Danny Brough, won the BARLA National Cup when they beat a brave, but outgunned young Wath Brow Hornets team, in the final played at Fylde Rugby Union club (current home of the Blackpool Panthers Rugby League club). East Hull wrapped up the National Conference League Premier Division title by defeating Leigh Miners in the play-off final staged at Featherstone. Leigh Miners had again finished as league leaders, but the power of East Hull - inspired by prop Lee Brown - got them home in the play-offs.

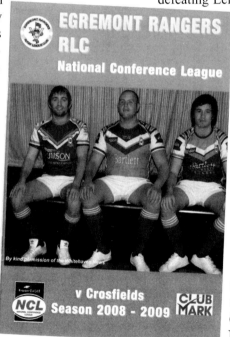

(Above) An illustration of the Amateur game in 2008 - as Egremont Rangers proudly give front-page treatment to three of their newest internationals who all represented BARLA Great Britain at different age-levels this year: John-Paul Brocklebank, Richard Farrar and Rhys Davies. Yet the trio are wearing three different jersey designs, none of which look anything like what most people would recognise as a Great Britain shirt!

York Acorn joined Wigan St.Judes and Thatto Heath in winning promotion to the Premier Division, and Acorn's Alfie Hill was named as the BARLA Open-Age coach of the year. In the second division of the National Conference there was a marvellous revival by Millom (the game's oldest amateur club) - they rose from the ashes to win their divisional Championship and win promotion. One of the strongest Amateur clubs in 2008 was Bank Quay Bulls (from Warrington.) They won the North West Counties League and then defeated Cumbrians Ellenborough to be crowned "Champion of Champions." The tremendous spirit of volunteers in the Amateur game was recognised when BARLA awarded life membership in 2008 to: Jean Girvin (North West Counties League), Lol Lowe (Wigan St.Judes), Roger Blair (Cumberland League) and Alfrida Kindon (Eccles and Manchester Amateur League.)

BARLA NATIONAL CONFERENCE LEAGUE
THE GRASSROOTS OF THE GAME

Take a look at the programme covers illustrated on this page and you will see a glimpse of another world in Rugby League. For the vast majority of people who only know the professional ranks it will be a largely unknown world - one that does not enjoy the wider media spotlight, but a world that effectively provides the foundations on which Rugby League is built.

The Amateur clubs have always been the real grassroots of the game and the programmes pictured come from their flagship competition, the National Conference League.

Flashback to the 1980s - as National League founder winners Heworth (represented by half-back Ian Ellis) tackle Thatto Heath, for whom Glyn Lewis has the ball.

The clubs illustrated are *(from top to bottom):* Stanningley, Eccles and Salford Juniors, Heworth, Siddal and Normanton. Don't be fooled by the modern-day "Australianised" add-ons of *Roosters* or *Knights* - these are some of the longest established Amateur clubs in the game situated in communities that have been immersed in Rugby League for many, many years. No sooner had BARLA been born and rejuvinated the amateur game in 1973, than one of their stated ambitions was to create an elite league for top clubs which would cross all county or regional boundaries and which would encourage standards to be raised, both on and off the field. It took until 1986 for the then called National League to get off the ground, in which ten founder member clubs set an example for all other BARLA clubs to aspire to. Others quickly wanted to join them and soon the League was expanded by public demand - now, called the National Conference League, it runs with 40 invited clubs playing in three divisions.

The BARLA National League 20 years ago in 1988, as the Bradford team Dudley Hill host Millom (from Cumbria). Dudley Hill's Steve Gorman breaks from the scrum chased by Millom's future Amateur international Mike O'Brien.

One of the National Conference League's biggest attractions for many supporters is the fact they play in the traditional British football season and they play their fixtures on Saturday afternoons - for generations who were brought up following the professional game that way - and see other major sports continue to do it so successfully - the attractions are obvious.

The very first winners of the National League in 1986-87 were Heworth, of York. Recent years have not been so successful for Heworth, but they remain one of the very few clubs to have been ever-present in the National Conference League from its inception to the present day. Another founder member, Millom, have also battled some tough times to re-emerge in fine style in 2008 and win promotion.

97

2008 - The year in Australia

In Australia 2008 was the Centenary year for Rugby League and the Aussies celebrated this milestone with great style and respect to those who had built the history of their game. The whole year was built around the Centenary with many promotions, exhibitions, wonderful books, television programmes, and the naming of various "best teams of the century" along with the official declaration of Australia's "best ever 100 players."

On the field, the Centenary would be marked by the 2008 World Cup after the end of the regular season, but on the date in May exactly 100 years on from the very first international match in Sydney between Australia and New Zealand, the two nations met again on the historic Sydney Cricket Ground. For this "CentenaryTest" both Aussies and Kiwis wore kits in the design of those worn by the pioneers of 1908 - Australia in the sky blue and maroon hoops and New Zealand the all blacks. It proved to be a magnificent spectacle.

True to form, the Australians won the Test relatively comfortably, 28 points to 12, after shooting away to a 22-nil half-time lead. The Aussies were captained by hooker Cameron Smith in the absence of the injured Darren Lockyer - Smith was one of six players from the Melbourne club in the victorious Australian team (albeit all of them Queenslanders) which was something few could have predicted just ten years ago, never mind 100 years back. The highlight of this "Centenary Test" was an incredible try created by the freak skills of Greg Inglis, playing on the wing that night - it reaffirmed Inglis as one of the mega-stars of the game in Australia in 2008.

GREG INGLIS - one of the game's mega-stars in 2008.

For two of those other so-called mega-stars, Mark Gasnier and Sonny Bill Williams, this was to be their swansong in Test match Rugby League as, not long after, they succumbed to the massive financial attractions of French Rugby Union clubs and declared they were heading for Europe. This new trend is another headache for the Australian Rugby League to face in its battle to retain its top players having seen so many others picked off by a cashed up Rugby Union in their own country and the ever growing numbers being taken by the big money on offer from the English Super League clubs.

There was an added poignancy to the "Centenary Test" as it kicked off little more than an hour after the death of Jack Gibson, the man elected "coach of the century" and acknowledged as such an influence on the game. As the game in Australia grappled with an ever growing problem of players misbehaving off the field (often alchohol related) - the words of Jack Gibson on the undesirable aspect of full-time professionalism and players not having day jobs to occupy them, began to ring more true than ever.

Australia's captain Cameron Smith lifts the Anzac Trophy following the 2008 Centenary Test versus N.Z.

The State of Origin series in 2008 was again won by Queensland, despite the absence of the injured Darren Lockyer, but the game so vibrant in the sunshine state was ready to enter a new era following the decision of coach Wayne Bennett to leave his position with the Brisbane Broncos and head south to St.George next year. Bennett had been the Broncos coach for 21 seasons, since they entered the competition back in 1988.

The N.R.L premiership in 2008 was won by Manly-Warringah, their first title since 1996. The "Sea Eagles" beat defending champions Melbourne in the Grand Final by an incredible 40-nil scoreline - something nobody could have predicted. Melbourne suffered badly by the abence of their captain Cameron Smith, controversially suspended for one of the dreaded "grapple tackle" decisions that caused such torment throughout the Australian season. It was the biggest ever winning margin in a Grand Final, beating the 38-nil result for Easts over St.George in the famous Langlands "white boots" final in 1975. Manly were inspired by their brilliant captain, scrum-half Matt Orford (a former Melbourne player), who also won the prestigious *Dally M.* award as the N.R.L.'s player of the year. The Grand Final was a major milestone for Steve Menzies, who equalled Terry Lamb's record of 349 games as the longest serving player in the history of the Premiership. Menzies has been a one-club man with his local Manly team since he made his first-grade debut in 1993 - he played for them in five Grand Finals and now has won two premierships with them. Now he has retired from the game in Australia and will be playing for the Bradford Bulls next year.

The Queensland Cup was won by the combined Souths-Logan City team, who beat Ipswich 24-18 in their Grand Final. The former Souths "Magpies" were one of Brisbane's most famous old cubs and this was their first premiership in 23 years.

2008 - The year in New Zealand

Rugby League in New Zealand had hoped to begin its second century in 2008 still on a high from the celebrations of its 100th birthday the year before - instead, it found itself struggling to overcome the blows inflicted both on and off the field in 2007.

On the playing front, the recriminations from the Kiwis' very disappointing Test series results against Great Britain in 2007 saw Gary Kemble's reign as the national team coach come to a very swift end. It was desperately unfair on such a decent man as Kemble to have to suffer the very public campaign against him led by the tour captain Roy Asotasi. That did Asotasi no credit, and in trying to put the blame onto Gary Kemble, nobody seemed to take into account the qualities displayed by the New Zealand players themselves on that disastrous tour or the fact that it was a Kiwi side shorn of so many of its established experienced players.

(Above, left) **MARK GRAHAM**, pictured in 2008 as he received the honour of being named New Zealand Rugby League's "player of the century."
(Above, right) **BRENT WEBB**, the Leeds full-back who flew to Sydney to play for the Kiwis in the Centenary Test against Australia in May.

The new coach, former Test forward Stephen Kearney (apparently with some advice from Australian Wayne Bennett) was able to select a much stronger Kiwi team for the "Centenary Test" in Australia in May - and, after a disastrous opening half hour in which they went 22-nil down, New Zealand managed to win back some confidence with a much stronger second-half. The inspiration for the Kiwis was the wonderful skill of loose-forward Sonny Bill Williams, who had appeared all too rarely for his national team. But, all too quickly, Sonny Bill was gone - lost completely to the Kiwis as he headed off to France to play Rugby Union.

Apart from a really good showing by the Kiwis in the World Cup, the one thing that could rebuild the morale of Rugby League in New Zealand in 2008 was always going to be some success for the Warriors - the Auckland based club side who play in the Australian N.R.L. competition, and who are very much the public face of the game in New Zealand. Sure enough - after many hiccups along the way in a topsy-turvy season - the Warriors produced the goods. After scraping into the play-offs in eighth place, they stunned everybody by coming up with a last minute win over top side, and defending premiers, Melbourne on their own pitch. That result meant a home play-off the following weekend against the Sydney Roosters - in a sign of just what a truly successful team could do for the game in New Zealand, all 26,000 tickets for that Warriors' game were sold within 15 minutes of them going on sale.

The Warriors are the public face of Rugby League in New Zealand. Pictured is winger Patrick Ah Van - who opted for Samoa in the World Cup.

The Warriors duly beat the Roosters in what was the farewell club game on New Zealand soil for their favourite son Ruben Wiki. There was to be no fairytale Grand Final for Ruben as the Warriors were beaten by Manly in Sydney in the semi-final. Much emotion was invested into the ending of Wiki's long and illustrious career, and there was to be one final curtain in an historic matched scheduled for New Plymouth in October between the "All Golds" and the New Zealand Maori. The Maori Rugby League Association were celebrating their own Centenary this year, and their team for this historic match was going to include Stacey Jones as well as Ruben Wiki.

Still on the Centenary theme, as New Zealand Rugby League announced its own team of the century, its accolade of the player of the century went to Mark Graham. Visibly humbled, Mark flew from his home in Australia to attend a special function in New Zealand to receive the award - the former great back-row-forward and Kiwi captain was a deserved winner as no individual did more to help change the perception of Rugby League in New Zealand from amateur game to an image of determined professionalism.

Next year, in 2009, the Auckland Rugby League (traditionally the strongest in New Zealand) will celebrate its own 100-year Jubilee.

2008 - The year in France

What a year of contrasts for French Rugby League in 2008. The good (*aka* the Catalan Dragons) was superb; the bad *(aka* the erosion of the domestic game in France) got even more worrying, with fears for famous foundation clubs like Albi and Villeneuve.

The success story of the Catalans in Perpignan rolled on to new heights; the Dragons achieving third place in the Super League; staging play-off games in Perpignan; and attracting capacity crowds to their Gilbert Brutus stadium which the local authorities now have "all systems go" to develop further to be able to accomodate even bigger crowds. Three years ago, before the Catalans had kicked a ball in the Super League, all this would have been just a dream - a wild fantasy - for the dwindling number of Rugby League die-hards in France. Now, the sky appears to be the limit for the Catalan Dragons, although a change of coach for 2009 will bring new challenges.

The major task for the Dragons, in their role as the vanguard for improving the French national team, would appear to be developing some good homegrown three-quarters - an area that used to be the strength of French Rugby League but, now, is its achilles heel. Despite the emergence of excellent forwards like David Ferriol, Remy Casty and Gregory Mounis, plus the rise of Thomas Bosc at stand-off, it was painfully obvious when France played England at the end of June just how much the Catalans rely on their Australasian imports for the match-winning quality they developed so well in 2008. The French went into that international with high hopes (despite their non-Catalan players being well out of season) but were swept away by the English to the tune of 56-8 in the stifling heat of Toulouse on a mid-summer's night.

In the domestic league competition, Lezignan emerged

Lezignan celebrate winning the Max Rousie Shield as French Champions after beating Pia in the 2008 Final at Beziers.

as Champions for the first time in thirty years - a joyous achievement for this small town in the *Corbieres* wine-growing region which remains staunchly a Rugby League town. Lezignan beat the holders Pia in the Championship Final staged in Beziers. In the Cup competition, another small town from the *Aude* region, Limoux, emerged victorious to take the Lord Derby trophy after a thrilling final against Albi in Carcassonne.

For Albi, in their first season back in the elite, that was a fine revival - led by second-rower Eric Anselme (who spent much of 2008 in England with Leeds) they went very close to winning the Cup - but the excitement soon turned to disaster when it became clear in the summer that financial problems were going to force the Albi club into administration. The thought of the famous *Racing Club of Albi* disappearing from the French Rugby League was a desperate blow to the game - for they, along with Villeneuve, remained the only two original clubs of those who started the game in France in 1934, to have maintained continuous active membership of the League.

Villeneuve themselves were facing an enormous financial struggle to continue, with a group of old players led by Daniel Verdes and Max Chantal trying to keep them afloat; whilst the once mighty Carcassonne survived their own financial crisis at the start of the 2007-08 campaign to go on and enjoy a good season, with their centre /second-rower Teddy Sadoui named as the French game's player of the year. In contrast to the struggles of Albi and Villeneuve there was the more positive news that Avignon would return as an elite club in the 2008-09 season - but the decision of Toulouse Olympique to abandon the French league and take up a position in the English National League One is likely to leave another large hole in the competition.

This was how the Toulouse club made amusing publicity out of their decision to take a place in the English League.

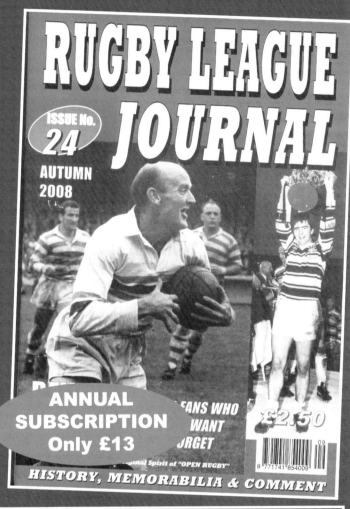

New Horizons in 2008

Rugby League certainly saw the promise of expanding horizons in 2008 as signficant achievements were reached by its professional clubs in all areas away from the game's traditional heartlands in the north of England. Both the Celtic Crusaders (from South Wales) and Gateshead (in the North East) achieved promotion from their respective divisions (Celtic via the licence system), whilst the Harlequins club saw products of London Rugby League's development schemes progress to becoming England squad members for the first time.

After so many years of struggle for the small group of Gateshead Thunder supporters, along with very loyal local North East players who have represented the club through thick and thin - notably lads like Kevin Neighbour, Robin Peers and Neil Thorman - it was heartwarming to see their new found success as Champions of National League Two. At Gateshead, as it also is in South Wales and in London, the game's major challenge has to be attracting more spectators to watch the game at professional level - however, in terms of player participation huge progress has already been made and is on-going.

By allocating a Super League place for the next three years to the Celtic Crusaders, the Rugby Football League are making a huge investment in the sport in Wales. The attraction of the gamble is that the potential of a whole country is being opened up to Rugby League - and, surely, among the youth of South Wales, there must be plenty of players who will be very suited to the League code. The early signs are good, with the Celtic Crusaders Colts (made up almost exclusively of Welsh players) winning, in very impressive style, the Rugby League's Co-operative Conference National Division (effectively the former Division Three); and the Welsh Under-18s winning a European Youth tournament in the Czech Republic (the one won last year in Serbia by the Whitehaven School team representing England.) No matter what the quality of the opposition, there's no doubt that a whole generation of Welsh Rugby League players is emerging, who can play the game comfortably and with confidence. The rest should follow. At the start of the 2008 season, Celtic Crusaders coach John Dixon said he would be happy if their Colts just managed to get a team on the field every week and fulfill all their fixtures - it was beyond all their predictions that the Welsh boys would be so successful, so quickly.

Junior activity and development programmes have been in place in London and the South East for some years now, and in 2008 all the hard work showed very real signs of bearing fruit as a host of local products played in the Harlequins first team. The fact that so many teenagers came through and were able to hold their own against other Super League teams was gratifying. Even more promising was the way the Harlequins reserve team, often

LONDON PRIDE - Louis McCarthy-Scarsbrook and Tony Clubb - two local products in the Harlequins side who proved in 2008 that they can match it with the very best.

made up almost exclusively of local southern boys, frequently put the cleaners through their counterparts from other well established Super League clubs from the north. And the icing on the cake, was the way Louis McCarthy-Scarsbrook and Tony Clubb established themselves as two of the Harlequins front-line players and made the England national team training squad.

More proof, if it were needed, that London-produced players can play Rugby League as well as anybody else, came with the oustanding form of the wingers Rob Worrincy (Sheffield Eagles) and Ade Adebisi (Whitehaven) - who were as good as any other English wingers running around in the Super League.

On the international front, a whole host of fledgling Rugby League nations continued to take their first steps in the game around Europe, with a variety of different tournaments and promotional tours. The potential for professional development still lies best with Russia, which now has had the game established for almost 20 years and where a little financial investment will go further than in many other countries.

The Student World Cup was staged in Australia in 2008, with the Aussies winning the title for the first time since 1996. The Australian Students defeated England 26-16 in the Final, with New Zealand beating Wales 24-18 in the play-off for third place. The other nations who took part were: France, Greece, Ireland and Scotland.

More international tournaments were being held later in the year - all in Australia to coincide with the senior World Cup - these included the third Women's Rugby League World Cup and the very first Police World Cup. Cambridge University also made a three-match tour to Australia, to mark the 20th anniversary of their first pioneering adventure down-under in 1988.

RUGBY LEAGUE'S ULTIMATE ROLL OF HONOUR

GREAT BRITAIN TEST PLAYERS 1907-2007

(Pictured) One of the greatest - Billy Boston in his Test debut in 1954.

THE COMPLETE REGISTER OF BRITISH INTERNATIONALS

Here and on the following pages we present the complete register of players who have appeared for Great Britain in full Test matches and World Cup games from the first one in 1907-08 to date (i.e. up to the very last one against New Zealand in November, 2007.) This register does not include matches against France before 1957, the year in which Great Britain-France games were given official Test match status.

KEY: After the player's name we list his total number of Great Britain appearances in brackets with a plus sign indicating substitute appearances, e.g. (5+2); the club(s) he was with, and the years which signify the duration of his G.B. career. *The letters "R.D." indicate the thirteen men who played in the legendary "Rorke's Drift" Test in 1914.*

A

ACKERLEY, Alvin (2) Halifax: 1952-1958.
ADAMS, Les (1) Leeds: 1932.
ADAMS, Mick (11+2) Widnes: 1979-1984.
ANDERSON, Paul (+10) Bradford: 1999 - 2003
ARKWRIGHT, Chris (+2) St.Helens: 1985.
ARKWRIGHT, Jack (6) Warrington: 1936-1937.
ARMITT, Tommy (8) Swinton: 1933-1937.
ASHBY, Ray (2) Liverpool City & Wigan: 1964 - 1965.
ASHCROFT, Ernest (11) Wigan: 1947 - 1954.

Great Britain Players Register - 2

ASHCROFT, Kevin (5+1) Leigh & Warrington: 1968-1974.
ASHTON, Eric (26) Wigan: 1957-1963.
ASHURST, Bill (3) Wigan: 1971-1972.
ASKIN, Tommy (6) Featherstone Rovers: 1928.
ASPINALL, Willie (1) Warrington: 1966.
ASTON, Len (3) St.Helens: 1947.
ASTON, Mark (+1) Sheffield Eagles: 1991.
ATCHESON, Paul (2+1) St.Helens: 1997.
ATKINSON, Arthur (11) Castleford: 1929-1936.
ATKINSON, John (26) Leeds: 1968-1980.
AVERY, Bert (4) Oldham: 1910-1911

B

BACON, Jim (11) Leeds: 1920-1926.
BAILEY, Ryan (+4) Leeds: 2004.
BARENDS, David (2) Bradford: 1979.
BARTON, Frank (1) Wigan: 1951.
BARTON, John (2) Wigan: 1960-1961.
BASNETT, John (2) Widnes: 1984 - 1986.
BASSETT, Arthur (2) Halifax: 1946.
BATEMAN, Allan (1+2) Warrington: 1992-1994.
BATES, Alan (2+2) Dewsbury: 1974.
BATTEN, Billy (10) Hunslet & Hull: 1907-1921.
BATTEN, Eric (4) Bradford: 1946-1947.
BATTEN, Ray (3) Leeds: 1969-1973.
BAXTER, Johnnie (1) Rochdale Hornets: 1907.
BEAMES, Jack (2) Halifax: 1921.
BEARDMORE, Kevin (13+1) Castleford: 1984-1990.
BELSHAW, Billy (8) Liverpool St. & Warrington: 1936-1937.
BENNETT, Jack (7) Rochdale & Wigan: 1924-1926.
BENTHAM, Billy (2) Broughton Rangers: 1924.
BENTHAM, Nat (10) Wigan Highfield, Halifax and Warrington: 1928-1929.
BENTLEY, John (2) Leeds and Halifax: 1992-1994.
BENTLEY, Keith (1) Widnes: 1980.
BENYON, Billy (5+1) St.Helens: 1971-1972.
BETTS, Denis (30+2) Wigan & Auckland Warr.: 1990-1999.
BEVAN, Dai (1) Wigan: 1952.
BEVAN, John (6) Warrington: 1974-1978.
BEVERLEY, Harry (6) Hunslet & Halifax: 1936-1937.
BIBB, Chris (1) Featherstone Rovers: 1990.
BIRCH, Jim (1) Leeds: 1907.
BISHOP, David (+1) Hull K.R.: 1990.
BISHOP, Tommy (15) St.Helens: 1966-1969.
BLAN, Billy (3) Wigan: 1951.
BLINKHORN, Tom (1) Warrington: 1929.
BOLTON, David (23) Wigan: 1957-1963.
BOSTON, Billy (31) Wigan: 1954-1963.
BOTT, Charlie (1) Oldham: 1966.
BOWDEN, Jim (3) Huddersfield: 1954.
BOWEN, Frank (3) St.Helens Recs.: 1928.
BOWMAN, Eddie (4) Workington Town: 1977.

(Above) IAN BROOKE and ALAN BUCKLEY playing in the 1966 Ashes in Australia.

BOWMAN, Harold (8) Hull: 1924-1929.
BOWMAN, Ken (3) Huddersfield: 1962-1963.
BOYLEN, Frank (1) Hull: 1908.
BRADSHAW, Tommy (6) Wigan: 1947-1950.
BRIDGES, John "Keith" (3) Featherstone Rovers: 1974.
BRIERS, Lee (1) Warrington: 2001.
BRIGGS, Brian (1) Huddersfield: 1954
BROADBENT, Paul (8) Sheffield Eagles: 1996-1997.
BROGDEN, Stanley (16) Huddersfield & Leeds: 1929-1937.
BROOKE, Ian (13) Bradford & Wakefield: 1966-1968.
BROOKS, Ernest (3) Warrington: 1908.
BROUGH, Albert (2) Oldham: 1924.
BROUGH, Jim (5) Leeds: 1928-1936.
BROWN, Gordon (6) Leeds: 1954-1955.
BRYANT, Bill (4+1) Castleford:1964-1967.
BUCKLEY, Alan (7) Swinton: 1963-1966.
BURGESS, Bill Snr. (16) Barrow: 1924-1929.
BURGESS, Bill Jnr. (14) Barrow: 1962-1969.
BURGESS, Sam (1+1) Bradford: 2007.
BURGHAM, Oliver (1) Halifax: 1911.
BURKE, Mick (14+1) Widnes: 1980-1986.
BURNELL, Alf (3) Hunslet: 1951-1954.
BURROW, Rob (4 +1) Leeds: 2005-2007.
BURTON, Chris (8+1) Hull K.R.: 1982-1987.
BURWELL, Alan (7+1) Hull K.R.: 1967-1969.
BUTTERS, Fred (2) Swinton: 1929.

C

CAIRNS, David (2) Barrow: 1984.
CAMILLERI, Chris (2) Barrow: 1980.
CARLTON, Frank (2) St.Helens & Wigan: 1958-1962.

CARNEY, Brian (14) Wigan & Newcastle Knights: 2003-2007.
CARR, Charlie (7) Barrow: 1924-1926.
CARTWRIGHT, Joe (7) Leigh: 1920-1921.
CARVELL, Gareth (+2) Hull: 2007.
CASE, Brian (6+1) Wigan: 1984-1988.
CASEY, Len (12+2) Hull K.R. & Bradford: 1977-1983.
CASSIDY, Mick (1+3) Wigan: 1994-1997.
CASTLE, Frank (4) Barrow: 1952-1954.
CHALLINOR, Jim (3) Warrington: 1958-1960.
CHARLTON, Paul (18+1) Workington & Salford: 1965-1974.
CHERRINGTON, Norman (1) Wigan: 1960.
CHILCOTT, Jack (3) *R.D.* (Huddersfield): 1914.
CHISNALL, David (2) Leigh: 1970.
CHISNALL, Eric (4) St.Helens: 1974.
CLAMPITT, James (3) Broughton Rangers: 1907-1914.
CLARK, Douglas (11) *R.D.* Huddersfield: 1911-1920.
CLARK, Garry (3) Hull K.R.: 1984-1985.
CLARK, Mick (5) Leeds: 1968.
CLARKE, Colin (7) Wigan: 1965-1973.
CLARKE, Jon (2) Warrington: 2007.
CLARKE, Phil (15+1) Wigan: 1990-1994.
CLAWSON, Terry (14) Featherstone Rovers, Leeds and Oldham: 1962-1974.
CLOSE, Don (1) Huddersfield: 1967.
COLDRICK, Percy (4) *R.D.* Wigan: 1914.
COLEY, Andy (1) Salford: 2007.
COLLIER, Frank (2) Wigan & Widnes: 1963-1964.
CONNOLLY, Gary (28+3) St.Helens, Wigan and Leeds: 1991-2003.
CORDLE, Gerald (1) Bradford: 1990.
COULMAN, Mike (2+1) Salford: 1971.
COURTNEY, Neil (+1) Warrington: 1982.
COVERDALE, Bob (4) Hull: 1954
COWIE, Neil (3) Wigan: 1993- 1998.

Great Britain Players Register - 3

CRACKNELL, Dick (2) Huddrsfield: 1951.
CRANE, Mick (1) Hull: 1982.
CREASSER, David (2+2) Leeds:1985-1988.
CROOKS, Lee (17+2) Hull, Leeds & Castleford: 1982-1994.
CROSTON, Jim (1) Castleford: 1937
CROWTHER, Hector (1) Hunslet: 1929.
CUMMINS, Francis (3) Leeds: 1998-1999.
CUNLIFFE, Billy (11) Warrington: 1920-1926.
CUNLIFFE, Jack (4) Wigan: 1950-1954.
CUNNIFFE, Bernard (1) Castleford: 1937.
CUNNINGHAM, Eddie (1) St.Helens: 1978.
CUNNINGHAM, Keiron (16) St.Helens: 1996-2006.
CURRAN, George (6) Salford: 1946-1948.
CURRIER, Andy (2) Widnes: 1989-1993.
CURZON, Ephraim (1) Salford: 1910.

D

DAGNALL, Bob (4) St.Helens: 1961-1965.
DALGREEN, John (1) Fulham: 1982.
DANBY, Tom (3) Salford: 1950.
DANIELS, Arthur (3) Halifax: 1952-1955.
DANNATT, Andy (3) Hull: 1985-1991.
DARWELL, Joe (5) Leigh: 1924.
DAVIES, Alan (20) Oldham: 1955-1960.
DAVIES, Billy (1) Swinton: 1968.
DAVIES, Billy J. (1) Castleford: 1933.
DAVIES, Evan (3) Oldham: 1920.
DAVIES, Jim (2) Huddersfield: 1911.
DAVIES, Jonathan (12+1) Widnes & Warrington: 1990-1994.
DAVIES, Will T. (1) Halifax: 1911.
DAVIES, William A. (2) *R.D.* Leeds: 1914.
DAVIES, Willie T.H. (3) Bradford: 1946-1947.
DAWSON, Edgar (1) York: 1956.
DEACON, Paul (10+1) Bradford: 2001-2005.
DERMOTT, Martin (11) Wigan: 1990-1993.
DEVEREUX, John (6+2) Widnes:1992-1993.
DICK, Kevin (2) Leeds: 1980.
DICKENSON, George (1) Warrington: 1908.
DICKINSON, Roy (2) Leeds: 1985.
DINGSDALE, Billy (3) Warrington: 1929-1933.
DISKIN, Matt (1) Leeds: 2004.
DIVORTY, Gary (2) Hull: 1985.
DIXON, Colin (12+2) Halifax & Salford: 1968 - 1974.
DIXON, Malcolm (2) Featherstone Rovers: 1962 - 1964.
DIXON, Paul (11+4) Halifax & Leeds: 1987 - 1992.
DOCKAR, Alec (1) Hull K.R.: 1947.
DONLAN, Steve (+2) Leigh: 1984.
DRAKE, Bill (1) Hull: 1962
DRAKE, Jim (1) Hull: 1960.
DRUMMOND, Des (24) Leigh & Warrington: 1980 - 1988.
DUANE, Ronnie (3) Warrington: 1983 - 1984.
DUTTON, Ray (6) Widnes: 1970.

(Above) JIM DRAKE pictured in his solitary Test for Great Britain against France in 1960. In support are TOMMY HARRIS, MICK SULLIVAN and DAVID BOLTON.

DWYER, Bernard (+1) Bradford: 1996.
DYL, Les (11) Leeds: 1974 - 1982.
DYSON, Frank (1) Huddersfield: 1959.

E

EASTWOOD, Paul (13) Hull: 1990 - 1992.
ECCLES, Bob (1) Warrington: 1982.
ECCLES, Percy (1) Halifax: 1907.
ECKERSLEY, David (2+2) St.Helens: 1973 - 1974.
EDGAR, Brian (11) Workington Town: 1958 - 1966.
EDWARDS, Alan (7) Salford: 1936 - 1937.
EDWARDS, Derek (3+2) Castleford: 1968 - 1971.
EDWARDS, Shaun (32+4) Wigan: 1985 - 1994.
EGAN, Joe (14) Wigan: 1946 - 1950.
ELLABY, Alf (13) St.Helens: 1928 - 1933.
ELLIS, Gareth (14+3) Wakefield Trinity & Leeds: 2003 - 2007.
ELLIS, Kevin (+1) Warrington: 1991.
ELLIS, St.John (+3) Castleford: 1991-1994.
ELWELL, Keith (3) Widnes: 1977 - 1980.
ENGLAND, Keith (6+5) Castleford: 1987 - 1991.
EVANS, Bryn (10) Swinton: 1926 - 1933.
EVANS, Frank (4) Swinton: 1924.
EVANS, Jack (4) Hunslet: 1951- 1952.
EVANS, Jack (3) Swinton: 1926.
EVANS, Roy (4) Wigan: 1961 - 1962.
EVANS, Steve (7+3) Featherstone & Hull: 1979 - 1982.
EYRE, Ken (1) Hunslet: 1965.
EYRES, Richard (3+6) Widnes: 1989 - 1993.

F

FA'ASAVALU, Maurie (+2) St.Helens:2007.
FAIRBAIRN, George (17) Wigan & Hull K.R.: 1977 - 1982.
FAIRBANK, Karl (10+6) Bradford: 1987 - 1994.
FAIRCLOUGH, Les (6) St.Helens: 1926 - 1929.
FARRAR, Vince (1) Hull: 1978.
FARRELL, Andrew (34) Wigan: 1993 - 2004.
FEATHERSTONE, Jimmy (6) Warrington: 1948 - 1952.
FEETHAM, Jack (8) Hull K.R. & Salford: 1929 - 1933.
FIELD, Harry (3) York: 1936.
FIELD, Norman (1) Batley: 1963.
FIELDEN, Stuart (22+3) Bradford & Wigan: 2001 - 2007.
FIELDHOUSE, John (7) Widnes & St.Helens: 1985 - 1986.
FIELDING, Keith (3) Salford: 1974 - 1977.
FILDES, Alec (15) St.Helens Recs. & St.Helens: 1926 - 1932.
FISHER, Tony (11) Bradford & Leeds: 1970 - 1978.
FLANAGAN, Peter (14) Hull K.R.: 1962 - 1970.
FLANAGAN, Terry (4) Oldham: 1983 - 1984.
FLEARY, Darren (1+1) Leeds: 1998.
FOGERTY, Terry (2+1) Halifax, Wigan & RochdaleHornets: 1966 - 1974.
FORD, Michael (+2) Castleford: 1993.
FORD, Phil (13) Wigan, Bradford & Leeds: 1985 - 1989.
FORSHAW, Mike (8+6) Bradford: 1997 - 2003.
FORSTER, Mark (2) Warrington: 1987.
FOSTER, Frank (1) Hull K.R.: 1967.
FOSTER, Peter (3) Leigh: 1955.
FOSTER, Trevor (3) Bradford: 1946 - 1948.
FOX, Deryck (10+4) Featherstone & Bradford: 1985 - 1992.

Great Britain Players Register - 4

FOX, Don (1) Featherstone Rovers: 1963.
FOX, Neil (29) Wakefield Trinity: 1959 - 1969.
FOY, Des (3) Oldham: 1984 - 1985.
FOZZARD, Nick (+1) St.Helens: 2005.
FRANCIS, Bill (4) Wigan: 1967 - 1977.
FRANCIS, Roy (1) Barrow: 1947.
FRASER, Eric (16) Warrington: 1958 - 1961.
FRENCH, Ray (4) Widnes: 1968.
FRODSHAM, Alf (3) St.Helens: 1928 - 1929.

G

GABBITAS, Brian (1) Hunslet: 1959.
GALLAGHER, Frank (12) Dewsbury & Batley: 1920 - 1926.
GANLEY, Bernard (3) Oldham: 1957 - 1958.
GARDINER, Danny (1) Wigan: 1965.
GARDNER, Ade (5) St.Helens: 2006 - 2007.
GEE, Ken (17) Wigan: 1946 - 1951.
GEMMELL, Dick (3) Leeds & Hull: 1964 - 1969.
GIBSON, Carl (10+1) Batley & Leeds: 1985 - 1991.
GIFFORD, Harry (2) Barrow: 1908.
GILFEDDER, Laurie (5) Warrington: 1962 - 1963.
GILL, Henderson (14+1) Wigan:1981- 1988
GILL, Ken (5+2) Salford: 1974 - 1977.
GILMOUR, Lee (5+9) Wigan, Bradford & St.Helens: 1998 - 2007.
GLEESON, Martin (19+1) St.Helens & Warrington: 2002 - 2007.
GOODWAY, Andy (23) Oldham & Wigan: 1983 - 1990.
GOODWIN, Dennis (5) Barrow: 1957-1958
GORE, Jack (1) Salford: 1926.
GORLEY, Les (4+1) Widnes: 1980 -1982.
GORLEY, Peter (2+1) St.Helens:1980-1981.
GOULDING, Bobbie (13+2) Wigan, Leeds & St.Helens: 1990 - 1997.
GOWERS, Ken (14) Swinton: 1962 - 1966.
GRAHAM, James (+5) St.Helens: 2006-2007.
GRAY, John (5+3) Wigan: 1974.
GRAYSHON, Jeff (13) Bradford & Leeds: 1979 - 1985.
GREENALL, Doug (6) St.Helens:1951-1954.
GREENALL, Johnny (1) St.Helens Recs.: 1921.
GREENHOUGH, Bobby (1) Warrington: 1960.
GREGORY, Andy (25+1) Widnes, Warrington & Wigan: 1981 - 1992.
GREGORY, Mike (19+1) Warrington: 1987 - 1990.
GRIBBIN, Vince (1) Whitehaven: 1985.
GRIFFITHS, Jonathan (1) St.Helens: 1992.
GRONOW, Ben (7) Huddersfield: 1911 - 1920.
GROVES, Paul (1) St.Helens: 1987.
GRUNDY, Jack (12) Barrow: 1955 - 1957.
GUNNEY, Geoff (11) Hunslet: 1954 - 1965.
GWYNNE, Emlyn (3) Hull: 1929 - 1929.

(Above) NEIL FOX, won 29 GB caps in the decade between 1959 and 1969.

GWYTHER, Elwyn (6) Belle Vue Rangers: 1947 - 1951.

H

HAGGERTY, Roy (2) St.Helens: 1987.
HAIGH, Bob (5+1) Wakefield & Leeds: 1968 - 1971.
HALL, Billy (4) *R.D.* Oldham: 1914.
HALL, David (2) Hull K.R.: 1984.
HALLAS, Derek (2) Leeds: 1961.
HALMSHAW, Tony (1) Halifax: 1971.
HALSALL, Hector (1) Swinton: 1929.
HAMMOND, Karle (1+1) St.Helens: 1996.
HAMPSON, Steve (11+1) Wigan: 1987 - 1992.
HANLEY, Ellery (35+1) Bradford, Wigan & Leeds: 1984 - 1993.
HARDISTY, Alan (12) Castleford: 1964 - 1970.
HARE, Ian (1) Widnes: 1967.
HARKIN, Paul (+1) Hull K.R.: 1985.
HARRIS, Iestyn (12+3) Warrington, Leeds & Bradford: 1996 - 2005.
HARRIS, Tommy (25) Hull: 1954 - 1960.
HARRISON, Fred (3) Leeds: 1911.
HARRISON, Karl (11+5) Hull & Halifax: 1990 - 1994.
HARRISON, Mick (7) Hull: 1967 - 1973.
HARTLEY, Dennis (11) Hunslet & Castleford: 1964 - 1970.
HARTLEY, Steve (3) Hull K.R.: 1980 - 1981.
HAUGHTON, Simon (+5) Wigan: 1997 - 1998.
HAY, Andy (+2) Leeds: 1999.
HAYES, Joey (1) St.Helens: 1996.
HELME, Gerry (12) Warrington: 1948 - 1954.
HEPWORTH, Keith (11) Castleford: 1967 - 1970.
HERBERT, Norman (6) Workington Town: 1961 - 1962.
HERON, David (1+1) Leeds: 1982.
HESKETH, Chris (21+2) Salford: 1970 - 1974.
HICKS, Mervyn (1) St.Helens: 1965.
HIGGINS, Fred (6) Widnes: 1950 - 1951.
HIGGINS, Harold (2) Widnes: 1937.
HIGHAM, Micky (+4) St.Helens: 2004 - 2005.
HIGSON, John (2) Hunslet: 1908.
HILL, Cliff (1) Wigan: 1966.
HILL, David (1) Wigan: 1971.
HILTON, Herman (7) Oldham: 1920 - 1921.
HILTON, Jack (4) Wigan: 1950.
HOBBS, David (10+2) Featherstone, Oldham & Bradford: 1984 - 1989.
HOCK, Gareth (3+1) Wigan: 2007.
HODGSON, David (3+1) Wigan & Salford: 2001 - 2007.
HODGSON, Martin (16) Swinton: 1929 - 1937.
HOGAN, Phil (6+3) Barrow & Hull K.R.: 1977 - 1979.
HOGG, Andrew (1) Broughton Rangers: 1907.
HOLDEN, Keith (1) Warrington: 1963.
HOLDER, Billy (1) Hull: 1907.
HOLDING, Neil (4) St.Helens: 1984.
HOLDSTOCK, Roy (2) Hull K.R.: 1980.
HOLLAND, David (4) *R.D.* Oldham: 1914.
HOLLIDAY, Bill (9+1) Whitehaven & Hull K.R.: 1964 - 1967.
HOLLIDAY, Les (3) Widnes: 1991 - 1992.
HOLLINDRAKE, Terry (1) Keighley: 1955.
HOLMES, John (14+6) Leeds: 1971 - 1982.
HORNE, Richard (5+6) Hull: 2001 - 2007.
HORNE, Willie (8) Barrow: 1946 - 1952.
HORTON, Bill (14) Wakefield Trinity: 1928 - 1933.
HOWARD, Harvey (+1) Bradford: 1998.
HUDDART, Dick (16) Whitehaven & St.Helens: 1958 - 1963.
HUDSON, Barney (8) Salford: 1932 - 1937.
HUDSON, Bill (1) Wigan: 1948.
HUGHES, Eric (8) Widnes: 1978 - 1982.
HULME, David (7+1) Widnes: 1988 - 1989.
HULME, Paul (3+5) Widnes: 1988 - 1992.
HUNTE, Alan (15) St.Helens: 1992 - 1997.
HURCOMBE, Danny (8) Wigan: 1920 - 1924.
HYNES, Syd (12+1) Leeds: 1970 -1973.

I

IRVING, Bob (8+3) Oldham: 1967 - 1972.
IRWIN, Shaun (+4) Castleford: 1990.

J

JACKSON, Ken (2) Oldham: 1957.
JACKSON, Lee (17) Hull & Sheffield Eagles : 1990 - 1994.
JACKSON, Michael (2+4) Wakefield & Halifax: 1991 - 1993.
JACKSON, Phil (27) Barrow: 1954 - 1958.

Great Britain Players Register - 5

JAMES, Neil (1) Halifax: 1986.
JARMAN, Billy (2) Leeds: 1914.
JASIEWICZ, Dick (1) Bradford: 1984.
JEANES, David (8) Wakefield & Leeds: 1971 - 1972.
JENKINS, Bert (12) Wigan: 1907 - 1914.
JENKINS, Dai (1) Hunslet: 1929.
JENKINS, Dai (1) Hunslet: 1947.
JENKINS, Emlyn (9) Salford: 1933 - 1937.
JENKINSON, Albert (2) Hunslet: 1911.
JOHNSON, Albert (4) *R.D.* Widnes: 1914 - 1920.
JOHNSON, Albert (6) Warrington: 1946 - 1947.
JOHNSON, Chris (1) Leigh: 1985.
JOHNSON, Paul (9+4) Wigan & Bradford: 2001 - 2005.
JOLLEY, Jim (3) Runcorn: 1907
JONES, Berwyn (3) Wakefield Trinity: 1964 - 1966.
JONES, Dai (2) Merthyr: 1907.
JONES, Ernest (4) Rochdale Hornets: 1920.
JONES, Joe (1) Barrow: 1946.
JONES, Keri (2) Wigan: 1970.
JONES, Les (1) St.Helens: 1971.
JONES, Lewis (15) Leeds: 1954 - 1957.
JONES, Mark (+1) Hull: 1992.
JONES-BUCHANAN, Jamie (+1) Leeds: 2007.
JORDAN, Gary (2) Featherstone Rovers: 1964 - 1967.
JOYNER, John (14+2) Castleford: 1978 - 1984.
JOYNT, Chris (19+6) St.Helens: 1993 - 2002.
JUBB, Ken (2) Leeds: 1937.
JUKES, Bill (6) Hunslet: 1908 - 1910.

K

KARALIUS, Tony (4+1) St.Helens: 1971 - 1972.
KARALIUS, Vince (12) St.Helens & Widnes: 1958 - 1963.
KEEGAN, Arthur (9) Hull: 1966 - 1969.
KELLY, Ken (4) St.Helens & Warrington: 1972 - 1982.
KEMEL, George (2) Widnes: 1965.
KERSHAW, Herbert (2) Wakefield Trinity: 1910.
KING, Paul (1) Hull: 2001.
KINNEAR, Roy (1) Wigan: 1929.
KISS, Nicky (1) Wigan: 1985.
KITCHEN, Frank (2) Leigh: 1954.
KITCHIN, Philip (1) Whitehaven: 1965.
KITCHING, Jack (1) Bradford: 1946.
KNAPMAN, Ernest (1) Oldham: 1924.
KNOWELDEN, Bryn (1) Barrow: 1946.

L

LANGLEY, Jamie (+1) Bradford: 2007.
LAUGHTON, Dale (4+1) Sheffield Eagles: 1998 - 1999.
LAUGHTON, Doug (15) Wigan & Widnes: 1970 - 1979.
LAWRENSON, Johnny (3) Wigan: 1948.

(Above) A try for BRIAN McTIGUE against New Zealand in the 1960 World Cup

LAWS, David (1) Hull K.R.: 1986.
LEDGARD, Jim (11) Dewsbury & Leigh: 1947 - 1954.
LEDGER, Barry (2) St.Helens: 1985 - 1986.
LEWIS, Gordon (1) Leigh: 1965.
LEYTHAM, Jim (5) Wigan: 1907 - 1910.
LITTLE, Syd (10) Oldham: 1956 - 1958.
LLEWELLYN, Tom (2) Oldham: 1907.
LLOYD, Robbie (1) Halifax: 1920.
LOCKWOOD, Brian (8+1) Castleford & Hull K.R.:1972 - 1979.
LOMAS, Jim (7) Salford & Oldham: 1908 - 1911.
LONG, Sean (10+5) St.Helens: 1997 - 2007.
LONGSTAFF, Fred (2) Huddersfield: 1914.
LONGWORTH, Bill (3) Oldham: 1908.
LOUGHLIN, Paul (14+1) St.Helens: 1988 - 1992.
LOWE, John (1) Leeds: 1932.
LOWE, Phil (12) Hull K.R.: 1970 - 1978.
LOWES, James (5) Bradford: 1997 - 2002.
LOXTON, Ken (1) Huddersfield: 1971.
LUCAS, Ian (1+1) Wigan: 1991 - 1992.
LYDON, Joe (23+7) Widnes & Wigan: 1983 - 1992.
LYNCH, Andy (1) Bradford: 2007.

M

McCORMICK, Stan (3) Belle Vue Rangers & St.Helens: 1948.
McCUE, Tommy (6) Widnes: 1936 - 1946.
McCURRIE, Steve (1) Widnes: 1993.
McDERMOTT, Barrie (11+3) Wigan & Leeds: 1994 - 2003.
McDERMOTT, Brian (4) Bradford: 1996 - 1997.
McGINTY, Billy (4) Wigan: 1992.
McGUIRE, Danny (9+3) Leeds: 2004- 2007.
McINTYRE, Len (1) Oldham: 1963.
McKEATING, Vince (2) Workington Town: 1951.
McKINNEY, Tom (11) Salford, Warrington & St.Helens: 1951 - 1957.
McNAMARA, Steve (+4) Hull & Bradford: 1992 - 1997.
McTIGUE, Brian (25) Wigan: 1958 - 1963.
MANN, Arthur (2) Bradford: 1908.
MANTLE, John (13) St.Helens: 1966 - 1973.
MARCHANT, Tony (3) Castleford: 1986.
MARTIN, Bill (1) Workington Town: 1962.
MARTYN, Mick (2) Leigh: 1958 -1959.
MATHER, Barrie-Jon (1+2) Wigan & Perth Reds: 1994 - 1996.
MATHIAS, Roy (1) St.Helens: 1979.
MEASURES, Jim (2) Widnes: 1963.
MEDLEY, Paul (3+1) Leeds: 1987 - 1988.
MELLING, Chris (1) Harlequins: 2007.
MIDDLETON, Alf (1) Salford: 1929.
MILLER, Joe (1) Wigan: 1911.
MILLER, Joe "Jack" (6) Warrington: 1933 -1936.
MILLS, Jim (6) Widnes: 1974 - 1979.
MILLWARD, Roger (28+1) Castleford & Hull K.R.:1966 - 1978.
MILNES, Alf (2) Halifax: 1920.
MOLLOY, Steve (2+2) Leeds & Featherstone: 1993 - 1996.
MOONEY, Walter (2) Leigh: 1924.
MOORHOUSE, Stanley (2) Huddersfield: 1914.
MORGAN, Arnold (4) Featherstone Rovers: 1968.
MORGAN, Edgar (2) Hull: 1921.
MORGAN, Ron (2) Swinton: 1963.
MORIARTY, Paul (1+1) Widnes: 1991 - 1994.
MORLEY, Adrian (24+6) Leeds, Sydney Roosters & Warrington: 1996- 2007.
MORLEY, Jack (2) Wigan: 1936 - 1937.
MORTIMER, Frank (2) Wakefield: 1956.
MOSES, Glyn (9) St.Helens: 1955 - 1957.
MUMBY, Keith (11) Bradford: 1982 - 1984.
MURPHY, Alex (27) St.Helens & Warrington: 1958 - 1971.
MURPHY, Harry (1) Wakefield Trinity: 1950.
MYLER, Frank (23+1) Widnes & St.Helens: 1960 - 1970.
MYLER, Tony (14) Widnes: 1983 - 1986.

Great Britain Players Register - 6

N

NASH, Steve (24) Featherstone & Salford: 1971 - 1982.
NAUGHTON, Albert (2) Warrington: 1954.
NEWBOULD, Tommy (1) Wakefield Trinity: 1910.
NEWLOVE, Paul (16+4) Featherstone, Bradford & St.Helens: 1989 - 1998.
NEWTON, Terry (13+2) Leeds, Wigan & Bradford: 1998 - 2007.
NICHOLLS, George (29) Widnes & St.Helens: 1971 - 1979.
NICHOLSON, Bob (3) Huddersfield: 1946 - 1948.
NICKLE, Sonny (1+5) St.Helens: 1992 - 1994.
NOBLE, Brian (11) Bradford: 1982 - 1984.
NORTON, Steve (11+1) Castleford & Hull: 1974 - 1982.

O

O'CONNOR, Terry (11+2) Wigan: 1996 - 2002.
OFFIAH, Martin (33) Widnes & Wigan: 1988 - 1994.
O'GRADY, Terry (6) Oldham & Warrington: 1954 -1961.
OLIVER, Joe (4) Batley: 1928.
O'LOUGHLIN, Sean (7+4) Wigan: 2004 - 2007.
O'NEILL, Dennis (2+1) Widnes: 1971 - 1972.
O'NEILL, Mike (3) Widnes: 1982 -1983.
ORR, Danny (+2) Castleford: 2002.
OSTER, Jack (1) Oldham: 1929.
OWEN, Jim (1) St.Helens Recs.: 1921.
OWEN, Stan (1) Leigh: 1958.
OWENS, Ike (4) Leeds: 1946.

P

PADBURY, Dick (1) Runcorn: 1908.
PALIN, Harold (2) Warrington: 1947.
PARKER, Dave (2) Oldham: 1964.
PARKIN, Jonathan (17) Wakefield Trinity: 1920 - 1929.
PARR, Ken (1) Warrington: 1968.
PAWSEY, Charlie (7) Leigh: 1952 - 1954.
PEACOCK, Jamie (23+3) Bradford & Leeds: 2001 - 2007.
PEPPERELL, Albert (2) Workington Town: 1950 -1951.
PHILLIPS, Doug (4) Oldham & Belle Vue R.: 1946 - 1950.
PHILLIPS, Rowland (+1) Workington Town: 1996.
PIMBLETT, Albert (3) Warrington: 1948.
PINNER, Harry (6+1) St.Helens: 1980 - 1986.
PITCHFORD, Frank (2) Oldham: 1958 - 1962.
PITCHFORD, Steve (4) Leeds: 1977.
PLANGE, David (1) Castleford: 1988.
PLATT, Andy (21+4) St.Helens & Wigan: 1985 - 1993.
POLLARD, Charlie (1) Wakefield Trinity: 1924.

(Above) TOMMY HARRIS - Hull's Welsh hooker who won 25 Great Britain caps.

POLLARD, Ernest (2) Wakefield Trinity: 1932.
POLLARD, Roy (1) Dewsbury: 1950.
POOLE, Harry (3) Hull K.R.: 1964 - 1966.
POTTER, Ian (7+1) Wigan: 1985 - 1986.
POWELL, Daryl (23+10) Sheffield & Keighley: 1990 - 1996.
POWELL, Roy (13+6) Leeds: 1985 - 1991.
POYNTON, Harold (3) Wakefield Trinity: 1962.
PRATT, Karl (2) Leeds: 2002.
PRESCOTT, Alan (28) St.Helens: 1951 - 1958.
PRICE, Gary H. (+1) Wakefield Trinity: 1991.
PRICE, Jack (6) Broughton Rangers & Wigan: 1921 - 1924.
PRICE, Malcolm (2) Rochdale Hornets: 1967.
PRICE, Ray (9) Warrington: 1954 - 1957.
PRICE, Terry (1) Bradford: 1970.
PRIOR, Bernard (1) Hunslet: 1966.
PROCTOR, Wayne (+1) Hull: 1984.
PROSSER, Dai (1) Leeds: 1937.
PROSSER, Stuart (1) *R.D.* Halifax: 1914.
PRYCE, Leon (17) Bradford & St.Helens: 2001 - 2007.

R

RADLINSKI, Kris (20) Wigan: 1996 - 2003.
RAE, Johnny (1) Bradford: 1965.
RAMSDALE, Dick (8) *R.D.* Wigan: 1910 - 1914.
RAMSEY, Bill (7+1) Hunslet & Bradford: 1965 - 1974.
RATCLIFFE, Gordon (3) Wigan: 1947- 1950.
RATHBONE, Alan (4+1) Bradford: 1982 - 1985.
RAYNE, Keith (4) Leeds: 1984.
RAYNE, Kevin (1) Leeds: 1986.

RAYNOR, Gareth (6) Hull: 2005 - 2007.
REARDON, Stuart (5) Bradford: 2004.
REDFEARN, Alan (1) Bradford: 1979.
REDFEARN, David (6+1) Bradford: 1972 - 1974.
REES, Billo (11) Swinton: 1926 - 1929.
REES, Dai (1) Halifax: 1926.
REES, Tom (1) Oldham: 1929.
REILLY, Malcolm (9) Castleford: 1970.
RENILSON, Charlie (7+1) Halifax: 1965 - 1968.
RHODES, Austin (4) St.Helens: 1957 - 1961.
RICHARDS, Maurice (2) Salford: 1974.
RILEY, Joe (1) Halifax: 1910.
RING, Johnny (2) Wigan: 1924- 1926.
RISMAN, Bev (5) Leeds: 1968.
RISMAN, Gus (17) Salford: 1932 - 1946.
RIX, Sid (9) Oldham: 1924 -1926.
ROBERTS, Ken (10) Halifax: 1963 - 1966.
ROBINSON, Asa (3) Halifax: 1907 -1908.
ROBINSON, Dave (13) Swinton & Wigan: 1965 - 1970.
ROBINSON, Bill (2) Leigh: 1963.
ROBINSON, Don (10) Wakefield & Leeds: 1954 - 1960.
ROBINSON, Jack (2) Rochdale Hornets: 1914.
ROBINSON, Jason (12) Wigan: 1993 - 1999.
ROBY, James (1+6) St.Helens: 2006-2007.
ROGERS, Johnny (7) Huddersfield 1914 - 1921.
ROSE, David (4) Leeds: 1954.
ROSE, Paul (2+3) Hull K.R. & Hull: 1974 - 1982.
ROUND, Gerry (8) Wakefield Trinity: 1959 - 1962.
RUDDICK, George (3) Broughton Rangers: 1907 - 1910.
RYAN, Bob (5) Warrington: 1950 - 1952.
RYAN, Martin (4) Wigan: 1947 - 1950.
RYDER, Ron (1) Warrington: 1952.

S

SAMPSON, Dean (+1) Castleford: 1997.
SAYER, Bill (7) Wigan: 1961 - 1963.
SCHOFIELD, Derrick (1) Halifax: 1955.
SCHOFIELD, Garry (44-2) Hull & Leeds: 1984 -1994.
SCULTHORPE, Paul (24+2) Warrington & St.Helens: 1996 - 2006.
SEABOURNE, Barry (1) Leeds: 1970.
SENIOR, Keith (31+2) Sheffield Eagles & Leeds: 1996 - 2007.
SENIOR, Ken (2) Huddersfield: 1965 - 1967.
SHARROCK, Jim (4) Wigan: 1910 - 1911.
SHAW, Brian (5) Hunslet & Leeds: 1956 - 1961.
SHAW, Glyn (1) Widnes: 1980.
SHAW, John "Joby" (5) Halifax: 1960 - 1962.
SHELTON, Geoff (7) Hunslet: 1964 - 1966.
SHERIDAN, Ryan (3) Leeds: 1999 - 2002.
SHOEBOTTOM, Mick (10+2) Leeds: 1968 - 1971.

Great Britain Players Register - 7

SHUGARS, Frank (1) Warrington: 1910.
SILCOCK, Dick (1) Wigan: 1908.
SILCOCK, Nat Snr. (12) Widnes: 1932 - 1937.
SILCOCK, Nat Jnr. (3) Wigan: 1954.
SIMMS, Barry (1) Leeds: 1962.
SINFIELD, Kevin (7+7) Leeds: 2001 - 2007
SKELHORNE, George "Jack" (7) Warrington: 1920 - 1921.
SKERRETT, Kelvin (14+2) Bradford & Wigan: 1989 - 1993.
SKERRETT, Trevor (10) Wakefield & Hull: 1979 - 1982.
SLOMAN, Bob (3) Oldham: 1928.
SMALES, Tommy (8) Huddersfield & Bradford: 1962 - 1965.
SMALL, Peter (1) Castleford: 1962.
SMITH, Alan (10) Leeds: 1970 - 1973.
SMITH, Arthur (6) Oldham: 1907 - 1908.
SMITH, Bert (2) Bradford: 1926.
SMITH, Fred (9) *R.D.* Hunslet: 1910 -1914.
SMITH, Geoff (3) York: 1963 - 1964.
SMITH, Mike (10+1) Hull K.R.: 1979 - 1984.
SMITH, Peter (1+5) Featherstone Rovers: 1977 - 1984.
SMITH, Sam (4) Hunslet: 1954.
SMITH, Stanley (11) Wakefield Trinity: 1929 - 1933.
SMITH, Tony (3+2) Castleford & Wigan: 1996 - 1998.
SOUTHWARD, Ike (11) Workington & Oldham: 1958 - 1962.
SPENCER, Jack (1) Salford: 1907.
SPRUCE, Stuart (6) Widnes & Bradford: 1993 - 1996.
STACEY, Cyril (1) Hunslet: 1920.
STEADMAN, Graham (9+1) Castleford: 1990 -1994.
STEPHENS, Gary (5) Castleford: 1979.
STEPHENSON, David (9+1) Wigan & Leeds: 1982 - 1988.
STEPHENSON, Mike (5+1) Dewsbury: 1971 - 1972.
STEVENSON, Jeff (19) Leeds & York: 1955 - 1960.
STOCKWELL, Squire (3) Leeds: 1920 - 1921.
STONE, Billy (8) Hull: 1920 -1921.
STOPFORD, John (12) Swinton: 1961 - 1966.
STOTT, Jim (1) St.Helens: 1947.
STREET, Harry (4) Dewsbury: 1950.
SULLIVAN, Anthony (7) St.Helens: 1991 - 1999.
SULLIVAN, Clive (17) Hull: 1967 - 1973.
SULLIVAN, Jim (25) Wigan: 1924 - 1933.
SULLIVAN, Mick (46) Huddersfield, Wigan, St.Helens & York: 1954 - 1963.
SYKES, Paul (1) Harlequins: 2007.
SZYMALA, Eddie (1+1) Barrow: 1981.

T

TAIT, Alan (10+4) Widnes & Leeds: 1989 - 1993.
TAYLOR, Bob (2) Hull: 1921 -1926.
TAYLOR, Harry (3) Hull: 1907.
TEMBEY, John (2) St.Helens: 1963 - 1964.
TERRY, Abe (11) St.Helens & Leeds: 1958 - 1962.
THACKRAY, Jamie (+3) Hull: 2005.
THOMAS, Arthur "Ginger" (4) Leeds: 1926 - 1929.
THOMAS, George (1) Warrington: 1907.
THOMAS, Gwyn (9) Wigan & Huddersfield: 1914 - 1921.
THOMAS, Johnny (8) Wigan: 1907 - 1911.
THOMAS, Les (1) Oldham: 1947.
THOMAS, Phil (1) Leeds: 1907.
THOMPSON, Cec (2) Hunslet: 1951.
THOMPSON, Jimmy (20+1) Featherstone & Bradford: 1970 - 1978.
THOMPSON, Joe (12) Leeds: 1924 - 1932.
THORLEY, John (4) Halifax: 1954.
TOOHEY, Ted (3) Barrow: 1952.
TOPLISS, David (4) Wakefield Trinity & Hull: 1973 - 1982.
TRAILL, Ken (8) Bradford: 1950 - 1954.
TROUP, Alec (2) Barrow: 1936.
TURNBULL, Drew (1) Leeds: 1951.
TURNER, Derek (24) Oldham & Wakefield: 1956 - 1962.
TYSON, Brian (3) Hull K.R.: 1963 - 1967.
TYSON, George (4) Oldham: 1907 - 1908.

V

VALENTINE, Dave (15) Huddersfield: 1948 - 1954.
VALENTINE, Rob (1) Huddersfield: 1967.
VINES, Don (3) Wakefield Trinity: 1959.

W

WADDELL, Hugh (5) Oldham & Leeds: 1988 - 1989.
WAGSTAFF, Harold (12) *R.D.* Huddersfield: 1911 - 1921.
WALKER, Arnold (1) Whitehaven: 1980.
WALKER, Chev (+6) Leeds: 2004 - 2005.

(Above) CLIFF WATSON, 29 caps for the St.Helens cockney-born prop.

WALLACE, Jim (1) St.Helens Recs.: 1926.
WALSH, Joe (1) Leigh: 1971.
WALSH, John (4+1) St.Helens: 1972.
WALTON, Doug (1) Castleford: 1965.
WANE, Shaun (2) Wigan: 1985 - 1986.
WARD, Billy (1) Leeds: 1910.
WARD, Danny (+1) Leeds: 2004.
WARD, David (12) Leeds: 1977 - 1982.
WARD, Ernest (20) Bradford: 1946 - 1952.
WARD, Johnny (4) Castleford & Salford: 1963 - 1970.
WARD, Kevin (15+2) Castleford & St.Helens: 1984 - 1992.
WARD, Ted (3) Wigan: 1946 - 1947.
WARLOW, John (6+1) St.Helens & Widnes: 1964 - 1971.
WARWICK, Silas (2) Salford: 1907.
WATKINS, Billy (7) Salford: 1933 - 1937.
WATKINS, David (2+4) Salford: 1971 - 1974.
WATKINSON, David (12+1) Hull K.R.: 1979 - 1986.
WATSON, Cliff (29+1) St.Helens: 1963 - 1971.
WATTS, Basil (5) York: 1954 - 1955.
WEBSTER, Fred (3) Leeds: 1910.
WELLENS, Paul (19+2) St.Helens: 2001 - 2007.
WHITCOMBE, Frank (2) Bradford: 1946.
WHITE, Les (7) Hunslet: 1932 - 1933.
WHITE, Les (6) York & Wigan: 1946 - 1947.
WHITE, Tommy (3) Oldham: 1907.
WHITEHEAD, Derek (3) Warrington: 1971.
WHITELEY, Johnny (15) 1957 - 1962.
WILD, Stephen (1+1) Wigan & Huddersfield: 2004 - 2007.
WILKIN, Jon (2+4) St.Helens: 2006 - 2007.
WILKINSON, Jack (11) Halifax & Wakefield: 1954 - 1962.
WILLIAMS, Billy (2) Salford: 1929 - 1932.
WILLIAMS, Dickie (12) Leeds & Hunslet: 1948 - 1954.
WILLIAMS, Frank (2) *R.D.* Halifax: 1914.
WILLIAMS, Peter (1+1) Salford: 1989.
WILLICOMBE, David (3) Halifax & Wigan: 1974.
WOOD, Alf (4) *R.D.* Oldham: 1911 - 1914.
WOODS, Harry (6) Liverpool Stanley & Leeds: 1936 - 1937.
WOODS, Jack (1) Barrow: 1933.
WOODS, John (7+4) Leigh & Warrington: 1979 - 1987.
WOODS, Tommy (2) Rochdale Hornets: 1911.
WORRALL, Mick (3) Oldham: 1984.
WRIGHT, Darren (+1) Widnes, 1988.
WRIGHT, Joe (1) Swinton: 1932.
WRIGHT, Stuart (7) Widnes: 1977 - 1978.
WRIGLESWORTH, Geoff (5) Leeds: 1965 - 1966.

Y

YEAMAN, Kirk (2+1) Hull: 2007.
YOUNG, Chris (5) Hull K.R.: 1967 - 1968.
YOUNG, Frank (1) Leeds: 1908.
YOUNG, Harold (1) Huddersfield: 1929.

GREAT BRITAIN INTERNATIONAL PLAYERS

From left to right: Great Britain international players: George Fairbairn, Steve Evans, David Topliss, John Woods, Mike O'Neil, Paul Rose, Mike Smith, Des Drummond, David Stephenson and Brian Noble - at Headingley in the 1982 Ashes.

They also played for Great Britain - in the years between 1952 and 1956, five full internationals were played between Great Britain and France which were not exhibition games staged in other countries. The British Rugby League authorities did not give full Test status to internationals against France until 1957, hence all the players who represented Great Britain in those games between 1952 and 1956 have never had their names recorded where they deserve to be, on the official register of Great Britain international players. On this page we list all those players and record their number of Great Britain appearances in the internationals against France pre-1957.

BANKS, Billy (2) Huddersfield.
BARTON, Frank (1) Wigan.
BEVAN, Dai (1) Wigan.
BOSTON, Billy (1) Wigan.
BOWDEN, Jim (1) Huddersfield.
BRIGGS, Brian (1) Huddersfield.
BROWN, Gordon (1) Leeds.
CAHILL, Ted (1) Rochdale Hornets.
CASTLE, Frank (2) Barrow.
CRACKNELL, Dick (1) Huddersfield.
DAVIES, Alan (2) Oldham.
EVANS, Jack (2) Hunslet.
FOSTER, Peter (1) Leigh.
FOX, Don (1) Featherstone Rovers.
GREENALL, Doug (2) St.Helens.
GRUNDY, Jack (1) Barrow.
HAYNES, Gordon (1) Swinton.
HOLLIDAY, Keith (1) Wakefield Trinity.
HORNE, Willie (1) Barrow.
IVISON, Billy (1) Workington Town.
JACKSON, Phil (2) Barrow.
JONES, Lewis (2) Leeds.
KELLY, Bob (1) Wakefield Trinity.
McCORMICK, Stan (1) St.Helens.

Tom McKinney - who played in four of the five "non Test status" Great Britain v France internationals, more than any other British player.

McKEOWN, John (1) Whitehaven.
McKINNEY, Tom (4) Salford & Warrington.
NAUGHTON, Alistair (2) Warrington.
PARSONS, George (1) St.Helens.
PAWSEY, Charlie (3) Leigh.
PRESCOTT, Alan (3) St.Helens.
PRICE, Ray (1) Belle Vue Rangers.
ROBINSON, Don (1) Leeds.
SCHOFIELD, Derrick (1) Halifax).
SILCOCK, Nat (1) Wigan.
SLEVIN, Ted (2) Huddersfield.
SMITH, Sam (1) Hunslet.
SOUTHWARD, Ike (1) Workington Town.
STEVENSON, Jeff (1) Leeds.
SULLIVAN, Mick (2) Huddersfield.
THORLEY, John (1) Halifax.
TOOHEY, Ted (1) Barrow.
TRAILL, Ken (1) Bradford Northern.
TURNBULL, Drew (1) Leeds.
VALENTINE, Dave (1) Huddersfield.
WARD, Ernest (1) Bradford Northern.
WILKINSON, Jack (1) Halifax.
WILLIAMS, Dickie (1) Hunslet.

SO - DID YOU KNOW?
ANSWERS TO THE QUIZ QUESTIONS IN OUR 'CLUB NOSTALGIA' PAGES

Wigan the 1983 John Player Trophy winners, with Nicky Kiss leading their lap of honour at Elland Road.

(Left) TOMMY HARRIS of Hull, being helped off the field injured in 1959-60.
(Right) JOHN PENDLEBURY in action for Halifax on their way to Wembley in 1987.

Barrow: Salford signed Bill Burgess.
Batley: Tommy Martyn.
Blackpool: Chuck Wiseman.
Bradford: Keith Mumby in 1984 and Ellery Hanley in 1985.
Bramley: Jim Windsor.
Castleford: Malcolm Reilly, Steve Norton, Gary Stephens & Kevin Ward.
Dewsbury: Alan and John Bates.
Doncaster: Tony Fisher.
Featherstone: Steve Quinn, who was signed from York.
Halifax: John Pendlebury.
Harlequins: Charlton Athletic's "The Valley."
Huddersfield: Peter Ramsden.
Hull: Tommy Harris.
Hull Kingston Rovers: Phil Lowe.
Hunslet: Fred Ward.
Keighley: Keighley Albion.
Leeds: Steve Pitchford.
Leigh: Trevor Allan and Rex Mossop.
Liverpool: White with a green band.
Oldham: Griff Jenkins was the coach and they beat Hull in the Final.
Rochdale Hornets: Frank Myler.
Salford: Millom (in Cumberland).
Sheffield Eagles: John Kear.
St.Helens: Alan Prescott.
Swinton: The county of Devon.
Wakefeld Trinity: Ken Traill, and he got it to have a speaking part in the film *"This Sporting Life."*
Warrington: Mike Gregory, in 1990.
Whitehaven: Neville Emery.
Widnes: Keith Elwell.
Wigan: Alex Murphy & Bill Ashurst.
Workington Town: Piet Pretorius.
York: Ryedale-York.

The FINAL WHISTLE

THE passing of each year brings new milestones to acknowledge in the world of Rugby League; new anniversaries to celebrate and tributes to pay. As we prepared to say goodbye to 2008 and look ahead to 2009, several major events sprang to mind very worthy of commemorating. The biggest, of course, was the end of the first century of the British national team, which we have celebrated in the pages of this Annual. With that came the very first Kangaroos touring team one hundred years ago in 1908.

Fifty years ago, in 1958, Great Britain won one of their most famous Ashes victories after the most dramatic of all Test matches - the Brisbane epic in which captain Alan Prescott played almost the whole game with a broken arm, refusing to leave the field because his team needed him out in the middle. The year 1968 was one of those pivotal years for many of us of a certain generation, and in Rugby League it was also one to remember. That was the year of the famous "Watersplash" Final at Wembley between Leeds and Wakefield Trinity, its 40th anniversary celebrations this year muted by the passing of its most remembered figure, Don Fox. 1968 also saw a World Cup tournament in which the French team surmounted the dramas of unrest and riots in their own country to reach the Final against Australia in Sydney.

1978 will always be remembered for a magnificent Challenge Cup Final between Leeds and St.Helens, a year when my old friend Paul Fitzpatrick first started reporting on Rugby League in the *"Guardian"* - it was also the year when the Australians last lost a full Test series, going down two games to nil in France, and our own Stephen Bowes, along with Mick Murphy, was possible the only Englishman there to see it. I am very happy to say that both Paul and Stephen can still be found contributing articles to our *"Rugby League Journal."*

1988 brought that wonderful try by Mike Gregory - another who has very sadly passed away since our last Annual was published - in a famous Great Britain win in Australia; followed by the biggest game in the history of the sport in New Zealand, a World Cup Final at Eden Park. 1998 holds a personal memory for myself as that was the year I gave up publishing *"Open Rugby"* and another personal milestone has come in 2008 as my own hometown club Whitehaven celebrated its 60th anniversary.

Among the former players and officials who contributed so much to the history of Rugby League who have passed away since our last Annual, we pay our respects to: the aforementioned Don Fox and Mike Gregory; Duggie Greenall, Norman Field, Mike Blackmore, Eric Ashton, Alan Buckley, Jack Bateman, Billy Blan, Harry Bath, Jim Drake and Paul Barriere - the founder of the World Cup. We will never forget them.
With my thanks for reading and best wishes to you all.
The Editor

Additional copies of this Annual can be obtained by post from the address below, price £12.95 per book (post free.) Please pay by cheque/postal order made payable to "Rugby League Journal."

Copies of our previous three Annuals: 2006, 2007 and 2008 are all now availabe at the bargain discount price of only £5.00 each (post-free). Our first Annual for 2005 is now sold old.

RUGBY LEAGUE JOURNAL
PUBLISHING

P.O. Box 22, Egremont, Cumbria, CA23 3WA
E-mail: rugbyleague.journal@virgin.net   Telephone: 01946 814249
www.rugbyleaguejournal.net